THE SOUTH AFRICAN BOER WAR

The Trials and Tribulations of the Second Battalion of the King's Shropshire Light Infantry

Ivor Williams

AuthorHouse™ UK
1663 Liberty Drive
Bloomington, IN 47403 USA
www.authorhouse.co.uk
UK TFN: 0800 0148641 (Toll Free inside the UK)
UK Local: 02036 956322 (+44 20 3695 6322 from outside the UK)

Because of the dynamic nature of the Internet, any web addresses or links contained in this book may have changed
since publication and may no longer be valid. The views expressed in this work are solely those of the author and do
not necessarily reflect the views of the publisher, and the publisher hereby disclaims any responsibility for them.

Any people depicted in stock imagery provided by Getty Images are models,
and such images are being used for illustrative purposes only.
Certain stock imagery © Getty Images.

This book is printed on acid-free paper.

ISBN: 978-1-6655-8756-3 (sc)
ISBN: 978-1-6655-8757-0 (e)

Print information available on the last page.

Published by AuthorHouse 06/30/2021

authorHOUSE®

Contents

FOREWORD

Like the author, I grew up with a fascination for the South African war. Ivor Williams had seen the memorabilia in his grandfather's home. For me it was the home in which I grew up, with Zulu assegais and shields on the walls of the hall brought back by my grandfather, who had served according to the bars on his Queen's South Africa medal, in Natal and Transvaal.

Ivor Williams provides some interesting background on the origins of the county militia and yeomanry and the reorganisations of the Army which led to the formation of the King's (Shropshire) Light Infantry. He then takes us through something of an anthology relating to Regiment's deployment to and campaign in South Africa. In one section he touches on the departure of the Regiment's 4th Battalion, late the Herefordshire Militia, who were called up for garrison duty in Gravesend to release regular troops for South Africa. He also tells us something of the 2nd Battalion the Worcester Regiment which also deployed to South Africa.

In places, the author reminds us of the overconfidence, arrogance and ignorance present in some parts of the British Army prior to engaging with the tough and determined Boers, and the shock they received at being initially over-matched by troops who they regarded merely as farmers. As one who turned to a life of military service having learnt a work ethic, the need for self-reliance and initiative, and a strong appreciation for the land, a proper understanding of which is so vital to the farmer and soldier, I find this a particularly telling criticism. Over numerous deployments to dozens of countries, encompassing environments as varied as the arctic north, the jungles of Latin America, the deserts of the Middle East, the arid mountains of South Asia and the confusing urban jumble of the modern city-scape, one has frequently been reminded that those who live in the landscape understand it best and should be respected for that. The need for humility and a readiness to respect and learn from the locals is a is vital lesson from this little book that might be well learnt by today's soldier.

General Sir Adrian Bradshaw KCB OBE,

Governor, Royal Hospital, Chelsea.

INTRODUCTION

I was born on 25 February 1932 in Hereford, England, and was christened at All Saints Church, in Hereford. My mother and father were both born in Hereford, and all my grandparents were born in Herefordshire or Shropshire. As a small boy, I can recall seeing the memorabilia of the South African Boer War in my Grandfather Morris's home, and I recall the stories that he told. In the 1950s, I migrated to Australia.

I decided to research the military regiments in which both my grandfathers had served during the South African Second Boer War (1899–1902). My interest originated from attending a small, quiet service which is held each year on 31 May at the Boer War Memorial, located in the park adjacent to the Bega Showgrounds, on the Far South Coast of New South Wales, Australia. The memorial, a tall, grey granite, four-sided obelisk, records the names of the seven local men who lost their lives in the South African War. The records reveal that on 24 October 1899, eleven members of the Bega Mounted Rifles left Bega at 7 a.m. and by nightfall arrived at Nimmitabel. The next day they departed Cooma on the afternoon train for Sydney. The distance from Bega to Cooma is 110 kilometres.

On 23 December 1899, a second contingent of volunteers left from the South Coast, departing Tathra on board the *Allowrie* for Sydney. The memorial was dedicated on 4 October 1905.

> Erected by the people of Bega and District in honor of the Officers and Men, hailing therefrom. who took part in the Boer War, 1899–1900 The names of volunteers sent direct from Bega and District and those District men sent from other parts Killed or Died.

Laid within the foundation by the builder on 18 August 1905 were copies of the *Bega Standard*, the *Southern Star*, the *Evening News*, and the *Town and Country Journal*. The cost of the memorial was 350 pounds. It should also be remembered that in 1899, Australia consisted of six separate colonies, and the population of the Far South Coast of New South Wales would not have exceeded twenty thousand.

The Bega Valley South African war memorial, NSW War Memorial by Martin Butterfield.

War memorials record the facts and some of the views of the inhabitants that funded the memorials. A detail on war memorials worth noting is what the community considered to be essential, and for military historians the answer lies in their recording of army units and recruiting patterns, which have passed into history.

One hundred eighteen years have passed since the end of the South African Boer War, and since that time, we have had the First and Second World Wars. We are able to look at this particular war free from emotion or impartiality. However, with the multitude of Internet locations that advertise and have information for sale that fit their own preconceived views of what the public are searching for, we have later generations of historians who have interpreted these according to the fashion of their times. Television, with its simplicities, military typecasting intellectuals, and pontification, have had arrogant and injurious influence on the views of recent generations. TV producers have then adapted these findings to fit their own preconceived view of what the public expects, and myths have been created and allowed to pass into folklore unchallenged.

On Saturday, 20 May 1905, a brass memorial was unveiled in the Hereford Cathedral recording the names of Herefordshire men who gave their lives for their country in the South African War from 1899 to 1902. The memorial records the names of seventy-four men and the thirty different regiments in which they served. Today, when you view this particular memorial, note the deterioration of the lettering: the names are getting harder to read, and in time they will be lost and forgotten.

It should also be noted that later, another brass memorial was unveiled within the cathedral with eight more names of Herefordshire militia who had fought and died in the conflict in South Africa. To be more precise, there are two further memorials within the cathedral recording the names of those connected to Hereford Cathedral.

I find it difficult to understand why a small and isolated rural community from the Far South Coast of New South Wales that lost officers and men in the South African Boer War, has multiple memorials, yet a prosperous and thriving county like Herefordshire was unable to record accurately the number of its inhabitants who fell in the South African War and required two separate memorials in the Hereford Cathedral.

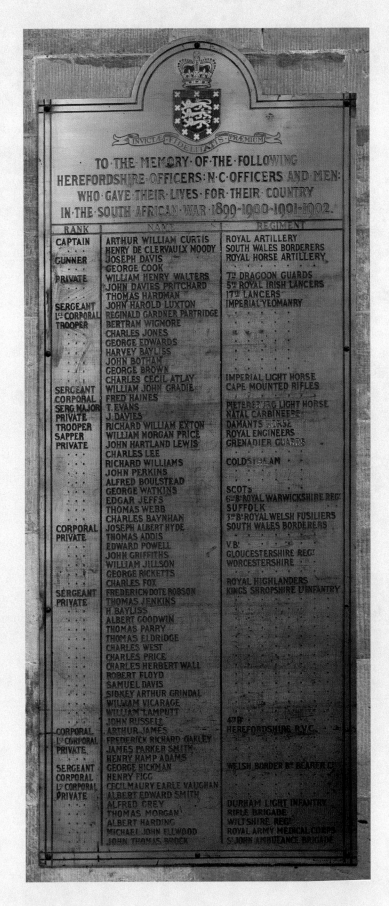

With kind permission of the Hereford Cathedral Library.

With kind permission of the Hereford Cathedral Library.

I have attempted to record the Herefordshire military history over the ages, including its involvement and contribution in the South African Second Boer War. The regiments involved are no longer in existence, and their records are scattered in various museums and the National Archives, Kew, London. It should also be noted that during the Second World War, Boer War army records stored in the cellars of the Guards Chapel in Wellington Barrack, London, were destroyed by a V-2 rocket. One of the tragic and unexplained occurrences that I found in the local Herefordshire newspapers were the reports of a number of returned volunteers from the Boer War having committed suicide shortly after returning home.

THE SOUTH AFRICAN BOER WAR, 1899–1902

On Saturday, 20 May 1905, in the presence of a reverential congregation and during a service of much solemnity, the Lord Lieutenant of the county, Sir John Cotterell, first Baronet, unveiled a nowy-headed rectangular metal plaque with incised inscriptions in black lettering in the Hereford Cathedral recording the names of Herefordshire men who gave their lives for their country in the South African War (1899–1902). Placed above the list of names was the city motto: "Invictae Fidelitatis Praemium."

It also said, "To the memory of the following Herefordshire officers, non-commissioned officers and men, who gave their lives for their country in the South African War, 1899, 1900, 1901, 1902."

This brass tablet contains the names of sixty-six men in some unregimental order, and these officers and men from Herefordshire were from thirty different regiments. The question that begs to be answered is why.

At a later date in 1905, another brass tablet was erected in the Hereford Cathedral on which is inscribed the following words:

> In memory of the men of the Militia Reserve of the 4th Battalion of the King's Shropshire
> Light Infantry, who lost their lives while serving with the 2nd Battalion in South Africa
> 1899–1902.
> Pte. A. GINGELL. Pte. C. LIMON. Pte. A. GOODWIN.
> Pte. W. VICARAGE. Pte. D. MOUNTAIN. Pte C. WEST.
> Pte. J. RUSSELL. L/Corp. W. S. MORGAN. (Died at Netley)
> This tablet is erected by their comrades.

For those of us in the twenty-first century seeking and searching for information about our ancestors' involvement and service in the South African Boer War, one cannot be anything but justifiably suspicious of an inflated class distinction in operation in Hereford, when in 1905 it required two brass memorials to record the names of the men who gave their lives for their country.

Why was it necessary for these heroes of Herefordshire to be distributed through thirty different army regiments to serve queen and country? I will try to find the cause of this apparent lack of regional coordination.

The Historic Record of the Thirty-Sixth of Foot, or the Herefordshire Regiment

The historic record contains an account of the formation of the regiment in 1702 and its subsequent service to 1852, when its fighting service career seems to have come to an end.

From 1852 to 1881, the army passed through notable changes, particularly in the organisation and interior economy of the British infantry of which the Thirty-Sixth formed a part and which ultimately led to its dropping the old number and old title as it was given a place among the defunct regiments.

Suffice it to say, the original formation of the Thirty-Sixth of Foot was not connected with the county. It was raised by William Viscount Charlemont in Ireland in the year 1702, and it was a marine corps, governed by naval laws on board ship and by military law on land.

Even then, it had its heroes and catastrophes, though they were not Herefordshire men. It was not till 1782 that a letter conveyed to the regiment, "His Majesty's pleasure that county title should be confirmed on the infantry and the 36th of Foot was directed to assume the designation of the Herefordshire Regiment, in order that a connection between that corps and the county should be cultivated, which might be useful in promoting the success of the recruiting service."

From that date to the year 1919, covering a period of 137 years, we have historical grounds for assuming that Herefordshire men have fought for king and country, and for justice, against a tyrant's boasted might both under the old Herefordshire colours and the new Herefordshire colours. We have no evidence to show the origin of the word *firm* nor the date when it was first adopted by the regiment, but it was prior to March 1791.

The reason why the Thirty-Sixth of Foot lost its old number, its old territorial title, and therefore its connection with the county of Herefordshire was that influential residents of Hereford partitioned the government not to establish an army military centre in Hereford.

The basis of army organisation was, and is, the cooperation with the principal authorities of the local administration. Its foundation was laid by the Army Enlistment Act of 1870, was shaped in 1872 by the localisation committee under Lord Cardwell, and was subsequently logically developed in the Mannon recommendations by another government in 1876, which gave a recommendation that was put into effect by yet a third government in 1881. England and Wales were parcelled out into ten districts, and commands were conterminous with county boundaries with a few exceptions, when two counties were joined together (like Worcester and Herefordshire). The bulk of the army and its organisation in territorial regiments today shows the principle feature of the army system.

When the Herefordshire Regiment in 1881 was reorganised, the following changes took place. First, the numerical designation of the Thirty-Sixth Regiment, which had been borne for 130 years, ceased. Second, the territorial designation of the Herefordshire conferred on the regiment on 31 August 1782 was changed to the Second Battalion of the Worcester Regiment, and the Twenty-Ninth Worcester Regiment would form the First Battalion of the Worcester Regiment. Third, green facing on the uniforms changed to white.

Not only had the old Herefordshire Regiment lost its county connexion, but the old Hereford County Militia has also been linked up with and became the Fourth Battalion, King's Shropshire Light Infantry. Then it merged with the Third Battalion of the regiment and ceased to exist as a separate unit in 1908.

THE KING'S SHROPSHIRE LIGHT INFANTRY

The King's Shropshire Light Infantry (KSLI) is the direct successor of two much older regiments, the Fifty-Third Shropshire Regiment and the Eighty-Fifth, the King's Light Infantry. The Fifty-Third was raised in Bridgnorth by William Whitemore in 1755, and in 1782 it was given the fuller title of the Shropshire Regiment. The Eighty-Fifth Light Infantry was first raised in Shrewsbury in 1759 and received its colours at the old St Chad's Church. This was the first light infantry regiment to be raised in the British army.

For over one hundred years, these regiments travelled and fought all over the world as two quite separate units until 1881, and with the British army reorganisation, two big changes occurred: there was a short service of recruitment, because up to that time, a soldier enlisted for life, and the barracks that had been built in Shrewsbury officially became the headquarters of the KSLI.

In May 1858, the government responded to a growing popular demand for the strengthening of British defences in the face of a perceived threat of French invasion by authorising Lord Lieutenants to raise volunteer corps under the provision of the 1804 Yeomanry Act. On 1 July of that year, Lord Palmerston's new administration announced that they would arm the volunteers with an issue of twenty-five Enfield rifles per one hundred volunteers on condition the corps provides a secure armoury and a safe range, adopts approved rules, and is subject to military inspection (Beckett 1982, 23–27).

With a persisting fear of French militarism under Napoleon III, 133 rifle corps were raised in 1859, attracting recruits at a rate of 700 per day, following by a further 578 corps in 1860—including Herefordshire's Thirty-Sixth in 1861.

The volunteer movement remained strong and numerous through the 1860s, 1870s, and 1880s, and it appears to have been quietly influential on late Victorian life. Nationally, it has been suggested it made a substantial contribution to the patriotic, moral, and militaristic values of the time (Beckett 1982, 197–203). Locally, the rifle volunteers could be a force for social change. In Shrewsbury, the need of the volunteers (often recruited among young clerks and solicitors) for target practice added to pressure for an early closing day.

It rapidly became a socially significant activity, and a county rifle competition held in Shropshire in June 1861 was watched by a crowd estimated at between twenty and thirty thousand (Dunham 1984). Musketry skill was paramount, and target practice—that interesting, healthful, and manly exercise which the rifle movement is supposed to supply—was seen as the main way of maintaining the enthusiasm of the volunteers (Beckett 1982, 113).

The Herefordshire Rifle Volunteer Corps were raised in 1860. Eight were formed in Herefordshire and three in Radnorshire; Company D was raised at Bromyard in May as the Fourth HRVC, and the volunteers started life as the Herefordshire Cycle Corps.

The War Office made these stipulations on setting up a volunteer corps. The force was liable to be called out "in case of actual invasion, or of the appearance of an enemy in force on the coast, or in case of rebellion arising in either of these emergencies".

While under arms, volunteers were subject to military law and were entitled to be billeted and to receive regular army pay. Members were not permitted to quit the force during actual military service and at other times had to give fourteen days' notice before being permitted to leave the corps. Members were to be returned as "effective" if they had attended eight days' drill and exercise in four months, or twenty-four days within a year. The members of the corps were to provide their own arms and equipment and were to defray all costs except when assembled for actual service. Volunteers were also permitted to choose the design of their uniforms, subject to the Lord Lieutenant's approval.

THE MILITIA OF SHROPSHIRE AND HEREFORDSHIRE

The militia was a form of home defence force whose ancestry can be traced back to the fyrd of Anglo-Saxon times. It was initially controlled and commanded by the sheriff, but from about 1541 it came under the command of the county Lord Lieutenant. In times of insurrection or invasion, the militia could be marched out of the county, but in all other times its area of service was within the county, and its expenses were met by the local owners.

This county levy was first styled as militia in the seventeenth century. Each county had an established militia quota, which was the number of men it had to raise if the militia were called out. In the seventeenth and eighteenth century, every parish kept nominal lists of men of military age who were required to do military service in time of invasion, warfare, or civil strife. These men were not volunteers. They had to do military service if called upon. for war. In every parish, a certain number of men were selected by ballot. The only way to avoid service was by providing a replacement, which wealthier individuals could do by paying someone else to serve in their place.

The militia was under the overall command of the Lord Lieutenant of the county (who also granted commissions to the officers), and the men would have to do an initial period of military training (up to three months) and then a set number of days for drill and training each year. Apart from that, they were free to follow their usual professions and occupations. Men trained in the militia were liable for service for up to three years and could be embodied (called up) for service at any time.

The system may be likened to a form of national service but of a more local character because the militia were not required to serve outside the UK, and their prime functions were as follows.

1. To provide a local defence force in case of invasion.

2. To provide garrison forces in important locations to free up regular battalions to serve aboard in times of war.

3. To supply regular units serving aboard with trained replacements.

However, in 1852 service in the militia ceased to be compulsory and became voluntary. Men could simply enlist into the Herefordshire Militia if they wanted a taste of army life, the glam of a uniform, the extra money from militia pay, the excitement of an annual camp away from home, and even the possibility of war service (but only in the UK) if war was actually threatened. In some respects, it was like an early form of Territorial Army at this time.

In 1881, as a result of the extensive army reforms, the Herefordshire Militia was linked to the King's Shropshire Light Infantry and was designated the Fourth Battalion of the KSLI. At the same time, control of the militia was taken from the Lord Lieutenants, and appointments and training came under the War Office.

THE OLD MEN

We shall peck out and discuss and dissect,
And evert and extrude to our mind.
The flaccid tissues of long—dead issues
offensive to God and mankind.
(Precisely like vultures over an ox the army left behind)

Rudyard Kipling

The Yeomanry

In the 1790s, following the French Revolution and the rise of Napoleon Bonaparte, the threat of invasion of the kingdom of Great Britain was high. To improve the country's defences, volunteer regiments were raised in many counties for yeomen. The word *yeoman* normally meant a small farmer who owned his land, but yeomanry officers were drawn from the nobility or landed gentry, and many of the men were the officers' tenants or had other form of obligation to the officers. At its formation, the force was referred to as the Yeomanry Cavalry. Members of the yeomanry were not obliged to serve overseas without their individual consent.

During the first half of the nineteenth century, yeomanry regiments were used extensively in support of the civil authority to quell riots and civil disturbances, including the Peterloo Massacre. As police forces were created and took over this role, the yeomanry concentrated on local defence. In 1827, it was decided for financial reasons to reduce the number of yeomanry regiments, disbanding those that had not been required to assist the civil power over the previous decade. A number of independent troops were also dissolved. Following these reductions, the yeomanry establishment was fixed at twenty-two corps (regiments) receiving allowances and a further sixteen serving without pay.

For the next thirty years, the yeomanry force was retained as a second line of support for the regular cavalry within Britain. Recruiting difficulties led to serious consideration being given to the disbandment of the entire force in 1870, but instead measures were taken the following year to improve its effectiveness. These included requirements that individual yeomanry troopers attend a minimum number of drills per year in return for a "permanent duty" allowance, and that units be maintained at a specific strength. Yeomanry officers and permanent drill instructors were required to undergo training at a newly established School of Instruction, and the Secretary of State for War took over the responsibility for the force from the individual Lords Lieutenant of the counties. These reforms improved the professionalism of the yeomanry force, but the numbers remained low, with only 10,617 men in 1881.

THE BRITISH ARMY AND THE
SECOND BOER WAR, 1899–1902

When the Staff College was established at Camberley in 1858, one of its main purposes was to remedy the appalling deficiencies that had been revealed during the Crimean War. Although the British army became stimulated by a profound interest in its previous campaigns, it also went off at a tangent, and after the Austro-Prussian War of 1866 and the Franco-Prussian War of 1870–1871, it turned its attention to the strategy and tactics of the Prussian general staff commander, Field Marshal Helmuth Graf von Moltke, to the exclusion of all others. In particular, it almost totally ignored some of the fundamental changes brought about by events in the American Civil War (1861–1865), and even though Sir Garnet Joseph (later Viscount) Wolseley, in his work *The Soldier's Pocket Book* (1869), stressed the importance of preparing for war in times of peace, it really only considered home defence. The army was still happy with its role campaigning against natives and tribesmen. The Second Battalion Hampshire Regiment, whilst in Ireland in 1897, still practiced forming squares.

The British commanders had indeed learnt the lessons of the Crimean War and could adapt themselves to battalion and regimental columns manoeuvring in jungles, deserts, and mountainous regions. What they failed to comprehend was that when they came up against the Boers, all their tactical and technical skills were of little use because they had entirely failed to comprehend the trench fighting and cavalry raids of the American Civil War, and in 1899 all the British service went to war with what was to prove outdated tactics—and in some cases antiquated weapons.

What the Boers presented was a new approach to warfare. The average Burghers who made up their commandos were farmers who had spent almost all their working lives in the saddle, and because they had to depend on both their horses and their rifles, they became expert light cavalry and skilled stalkers and marksmen. From their knowledge of the country, they could make use of every scrap of cover, from which they could pour in a destructive fire using their modern Mauser rifles. The Boers also had around one hundred of the latest Krupp field guns, all horse-drawn and dispersed among the various commando groups. Their skill in adapting themselves into first-rate artillerymen proved them to have been a versatile adversary.

The British army in 1899 was mentally and materially ill-equipped to deal with such antagonists as the Boers. True, the officers and men had seen far more active service than most of their continental counterparts, but it was largely irrelevant to the conditions of a major campaign against a skilled and determined enemy armed with modern weapons. What was more, the small wars which the British army were almost constantly involved in throughout the late nineteenth century tended to make both officers and men not only complacent but also rather arrogant in the face of what they considered to be a handful of rustic Dutch farmers who could soon be brought to heel by well-disciplined regulars.

The British infantry had already had a taste of what to expect during the First Boer War of 1880–1881. The crisis in the Transvaal at the end of the nineteenth century was the culmination of two and a half centuries of Afrikaner expansion and conflict with African and British forces. In 1880, the Boers, under Paul Kruger, rose in revolt over taxation and proclaimed a republic. Within a few weeks, they inflicted three but small but shattering reverses on the British army.

The hostilities began against a number of small scattered British army garrisons beginning with the siege of two companies of the 2/21st Regiment of Foot (the Royal Scots Fusiliers) at Potchefstroom and culminating in the battle of Majuba just inside the British territory of Natal. Responsibility for restoring order fell on the British commissioner of troops in Natal and Transvaal, Sir George Pomeroy-Colley, who was also high commissioner for South-East Africa.

On 20 December 1880, there occurred the first of a series of disasters. A party of about two hundred Boers, under Frank Joubert, annihilated a column of the Ninety-Fourth Regiment of Foot (the Connaught Rangers) on their march from Lydenburge to Pretoria at Bronkhorst Spruit. They were shot to pieces by the Boer marksmen, and the survivors of the unprepared column were ordered to surrender by their fatally wounded commander, Lieutenant-Colonel Anstruther.

Two features were especially evident in this action: the devastating Boer marksmen, which inflicted an average of five injuries upon each of the British wounded in less than fifteen minutes, and the kindly treatment accorded by the Boers to the defeated enemy once the action was over. Of the 263 of all ranks, including 40 of the band, 57 of the British were killed and more than 100 were wounded (20 fatally). All nine officers became casualties.

Some aspects of the action seemed to belong to another age. Before the shooting began, the Boers gave Anstruther the chance to surrender, and immediately before the fight, the Ninety-Fourth band played the national anthem. After the surrender, Joubert joined the fatally stricken Anstruther in toasting Queen Victoria, and as the unwounded were marched away, the survivors of the band played "Rule Britannia".

Sir George Pomeroy-Colley gathered some 1,200 men to relieve the several besieged posts in the Transvaal, but upon marching into the territory, he found his way barred by some two hundred Boers at Laing's Nek, and on 28 January 1881, they initiated the attack on the Boer positions. They dug in at the top of Laing's Nek with 180 cavalry, 870 infantry, 6 cannons, and a naval attachment with rocket tubes. They bombarded the Boer positions for twenty minutes before storming the hill. This was the last occasion in which British colours were carried into action by a British regiment, the Fifty-Eighth Regiment of Foot (the Rutlandshire Regiment). This attack was duly beaten off by the Boer riflemen with 150 killed in action. Colley retired to his camp at Mount Prospect to await reinforcements, but on 7 February, he had to strike south-west to drive away a three-hundred-strong commando unit under Nicolaas Smit.

At this juncture, the campaign was suspended by negotiations between Kruger and the British government. However, Colley decided to do something during the waiting for the Boer reply. He was reinforced by a column under Brigadier General Evelyn Wood, which included troops from India, the Ninety-Second (Gordon Highlanders). The Ninety-Second wore khaki, which contrasted markedly with the red and green uniforms of the other detachments. On the night of 26 February, Colley led a force to occupy the heights of Majuba Hill, which commanded the Boer position around Laing's Nek.

This force was composed of two companies of the Fifty-Eighth of Foot, two companies of the 3/60th of Foot (King's Royal Rifle Corps), three companies of the Ninety-Second Highlands, and a detachment of sixty-four seamen but no artillery. On the following morning, the Boers began to ascend the hill, and with accurate musketry and skill in utilising natural cover, they overwhelmed the defenders, some of whom broke and fled down the hill.

Of Colley's 365 men, 285 were killed or wounded, compared to the loss of two Boers killed and four wounded. Colley was among the dead, and Evelyn Wood assumed command. Following the truce from 6 March, terms of peace were concluded on 21 March 1881. The Cardwell Reforms came into effect on 1 March 1881, when the old Fifty-Eighth (Rutlandshire Regiment of Foot) became the Second Battalion of the Northamptonshire Regiment. The Ninety-Second became the Second Battalion Gordon Highlanders, the Sixtieth became the King's Royal Rifle Corps, the Twenty-First became the Royal Scots Fusiliers, and the Ninety-Fourth became the Second Battalion of the Connaught Rangers. The old colours of the Fifty-Eighth Regiment of Foot are on display at the Abington Park Museum, Northampton.

That nothing had been done to remedy these defects in 1899 is shown by the way that General White's force was caught at Nicholsons Nek on 29 October 1899, when the British infantry followed the same tactical pattern that had cost them so dearly at Majubu Hill. Despite this disaster, some British commanders still tried to dismiss their own shortcomings and attempted to place all the onus on the way in which the enemy fought. The well-constructed Boer trenches at the Modder River (28 November 1899) was over four miles long and was dug and concealed on the forward bank of the river. Together with others rising in tiers towards the crest of the hills beyond, they portended things to come in 1914–1918. The same thing was to happen over and over again with disastrous results during the first months of the war. The British infantry became pinned down without much cover and under the boiling sun, without an enemy in sight or the means of retreat.

If the British infantry had to learn the lessons of modern warfare the hard way, the British cavalry were also in for a shock when it came to putting the spit and polish of its classic cavalry methods into practice on the plains of South Africa. The cavalry officer class, perhaps above all others within the British army, was particularly slow to learn lessons of their own campaigns, to say nothing of not studying at learning from anything of the mounted tactics of the American Civil War.

Even with the more enlightened writings of George Henderson and Colonel George Denison, both of whom understood the changes that had occurred in cavalry organisation and tactics as a result of the American experience, the majority of cavalry officer class considered that they could learn nothing from a war in which there had been no cavalry charges at Gettysburg, that the skills of the British were enough to engage in one, and that nothing much could be done with volunteer horsemen who preferred the pistol and carbine to the sabre. The fact that regular British cavalry regiments had the carbine thrust upon them did not go down well owing to the extra weight, and they were reluctant to relinquish the lance, which if anything was even more of an inconvenience. This outdated weapon was still in service up to 1917, awaiting the chance to be used in the pursuit of a beaten foe.

In 1888, there had been steps taken by the War Department in ordering many of the county battalions to form detachments of mounted infantry because it was easier and quicker to train infantrymen to a basic standard of horsemanship than to try to retrain a regular cavalryman, who not only resented the task in the first place but also had the full support of his colonel in not wasting his talent on such unnecessary gimmicks. It was only after yet another blunder at Bloemfontein, where General Broadwood was ambushed in April 1900, that the skills of the British mounted infantry, together with the aid of their better-trained New Zealand allies, began to dawn on a few cavalry commanders. However, even this did not stop some like General French from criticising the fact that these units were crippling the army, especially the regular cavalry and the artillery.

The real irony for the British cavalry in South Africa was that it could have provided a real theatre of war for the demonstration of a well-trained mounted force. The great expanses of open terrain were ideally suited to wide, sweeping raids in which the Boer could have been fought on his own terms from the very start. Not only this, but the Boer battlefield tactics of digging themselves in and awaiting a frontal assault could have led to their undoing. Here was the chance to use the British cavalry to full effect.

With the arrival of the new commander-in-chief, Lord Roberts, or "Bobs", the British cavalry at last began to be used with some effect, and he recognised the need for a complete rethinking in cavalry tactics. "I think we might have done better on more than one occasion if our cavalry had been judiciously handled. Our mounted infantry has much improved of late, and I intend to see whether their employment in large bodies will bring about more satisfactory results."

That Roberts was a voice in the wilderness as far as the general feelings of most cavalry officers were concerned is shown by the remarks of then Major Douglas Haig, who, being present on General French's staff during the Boer War, considered that it was necessary to keep the cavalry in its old form because the charge was the ultimate aim of their training. Haig was still mooting these same sentiments even when he became commander-in-chief of the British Expeditionary Force in 1915.

THE ARTILLERY

As far as artillery was concerned, the British army should not have been playing catch-up to any other country in the world. During the American Civil War, British-made breech-loading cannons had been in use but were never in great numbers. However, by 1870 both Britain's home army and her army in India were fully equipped with breech-loading cannons, and although not perfect owing to gas leakages around the breech, they were nevertheless a great improvement on the old muzzle-loading cannons of the past.

Because of the poor performance of some of the breech-loading guns during active service in desert conditions, the new Ordnance Department, which had replaced the old Board of Ordnance in 1855, decided in its infinite wisdom to rearm the whole of the Royal Artillery with muzzle-loading cannons in 1871. Not even the outstanding successes of the Krupp breech-loading guns used during the Franco-Prussian War of 1890–1891 dissuaded the British army from returning to a weapon already rejected by every other modern army. By 1880, there were only two breech-loading batteries left, and these were in the army in India; by 1890, even these had gone.

What finally brought the army back to its senses were the problems pondered upon when considering an invasion of the British mainland. It was found that battleship firepower had increased, so the garrison artillery had to respond in a like fashion in order to keep pace. As guns became larger, the difficulty of using muzzle-loaders became more apparent, especially when gun crews had to climb up to swab out a massive casement-installed cannon each time it was fired and then reload at the muzzle. This was the deciding factor that made the British army once again revert to breech-loading cannon, but even with the outbreak of the Boer War in 1899, there were still one or two field batteries that had not been converted, like the Natal Field Artillery, which still used seven-pounder rifled muzzle-loaders.

No testing had been carried out prior to the outbreak of the war to compare the capabilities of the German-made Krupp field gun with that of the "much improved" British fifteen-pounder howitzer, and it was only after the first disastrous battles with the Boers that it was realised that the Krupp cannon outranged the British artillery, a damning indictment of the way the army went to war. What was more, the Boers had a weapon which the Ordnance Department had rejected as an unnecessary refinement in 1898. This was the Krupp "Pom-Pom", a weapon that the British soldier came to dread on the battlefields of South Africa. On more than one occasion, it took out entire gun crews and groups of infantries with its rapid-firing burst of twenty or more-one-pound shells.

The Second Boer War was not a "small war" in which the British army was able to defeat and subdue a semi backwards enemy according to its training. The war in South Africa grew into a serious conflict, and though it brought volunteers from every part of the Empire to the assistance of the mother country, it seriously strained its resources and exhibited to the military critics on the continent of Europe the numerous shortcomings of the British army.

Although it was the Boers who had declared war, the sympathy of the continent was behind the Boers. The skill and tenacity with which a group of farmers had resisted the professional forces of a great empire were very much admired. To distant observers, the war must have appeared as a contest between liberty and despotism, and every victory of the Boers was received with rapturous enthusiasm by both the French and the Germans; even the Tsar of Russia, whose own domestic government was no model for freedom, proposed a general alliance of the continental powers against Britain.

The war was declared by the Transvaal government with the support of the Orange Free State on 11 October 1899, and the two regiments that we are interested in, the Second. Battalion, the King's Shropshire Light Infantry and the Second Battalion, Worcester Regiment, would have immediately recalled their reserves to the colours. At the same time, the Herefordshire and Shropshire militia were also called up for duty.

The Departure of the Herefordshire Militia

The official records of the Fourth Battalion of the King's Shropshire Light Infantry and their movement to Gravesend state the following.

> In pursuance of the proclamation of Her Majesty the Queen, in council, The Battalion was Embedded at Hereford on December 12th 1899. Heavy snow had fallen during the preceding night, which interfered with the assembly and clothing and equipment of the battalion, but in spite of difficulties the regiment was able to leave Hereford at the appointed hour 4.45 pm and proceeded by special train to Gravesend, which was reached at 1am on December 13th.

The *Hereford Times* recorded a more detailed picture.

> The embedment of the 4th Battalion King's Shropshire Light Infantry late the Herefordshire Militia, for garrison duty at Gravesend is certainly one of the most important events of the week. It denotes trouble—sometimes and how men are ready and willing to give their service for the purpose of home defence when their regular brethren are away on foreign duty and fighting in the country's name. The call up of the Militia is fortunately but a rare occurrence in these days, in so much as the military authorities only do as a last resort, irrespective of the volunteers. However, Herefordshire Militia are not strangers to the order, having rendered signal service in this direction on several occasions.

When the news spread about six weeks later that the battalion was expected to hold itself in readiness, no surprise was occasioned; in fact, such a circumstance was rather expected. Eventually coloured bills were posted in conspicuous places throughout the county ordering the men assemble at the barracks at Hereford at 10 a.m. on Tuesday, 24 October 1899, when everyone was required to be present, unless he received a notice absolving him from attendance. Recruits were also asked for, and old soldiers were requested to do their best to bring then in. The majority of the men were employed in the Welsh mining districts; others were at various distances from Hereford. It was anticipated that extensive arrangements would have to be made for their lodging, with there being limited space at headquarters during the time they were being served with their arms and accoutrements.

However, on Friday, the order came not to billet the men at Hereford, stating that they were to receive their uniforms and other gear on the same day of their departure. Naturally, there was a considerable influx into Hereford and the neighbourhood of the barracks on Tuesday was very busy. The battalion was rather behind its full regimental strength of 650, but with the aid of recruits, this deficiency was expected to be resumed. About 440 men put in an appearance, and much praise is due to the officials for the successful manner in which they were coped with. The general public evinced much interest in the arrangements, the wall lining the barracks was enclosed, being surrounding by people during the whole of the day. At about four o'clock, the crowd was huge.

The scene was a wintery one, with snow covering the ground, but this was relished by a number of men during their spare moments, who indulged in snowballing and all kinds of pranks. A certain section of men who were either elated at their going or wished to drown their sorrows at the thought of parting from wives, families, sweethearts, relations, and friends, appeared under rather amusing conditions. A little latitude must be given in view of the stern duty to follow. Several were troublesome and had to be placed in the "clink", which necessitated their making the journey the following day.

A chip potato van did a roaring trade on the ground, and the men's comforts were well attended to. We understand that Mr W. Pilley of Eign Street catered five hundred pork pies. At four o'clock, the bugle sounded, and six companies lined up in the centre of the ground. The following officers were in attendance: Colonel. E. Scudamore Lucas, in command; Major Bourne, second in command; Captain Symon-Taylor; Captain Catlow; Captain and Adjutant Judge Lieutenant Fernie; Lieutenant Croft; Lieutenant Cox; Lieutenant; Bird, Lieutenant Fatzjohn; Lieutenant; and Quartermaster Bailey. Captain Sharpley and Lieutenant Rowen had already proceeded to Gravesend. The roll call was read out, and subsequently various emulations were indulged in. Then the order came to form fours, and in this manner the battalion was marched to Barr's Court Station, headed by the Herefordshire Volunteers Band under the direction of bandmaster St John Jones, which played "Soldiers of the Queen" to a lively and brisk step. The streets were lined with townspeople and many from the country to give the departing ones an enthusiastic send-off. The neighbourhood of St Owen's turned out en masse and were particularly demonstrative when they recognised one of their comrades. The men themselves were distinctly jocular, and one individual shouted out that he only wished he could have the chance to pull old Kruger's whiskers—a remark which caused much laughter. An old gentleman who was an interested spectator thought that the Transvaal was more like Gravesend, the town the militia were proceed to, and fervently hoped the men would not be required to make the journey. That seemed amusing to many of the spectators, but there is a sad side to the end. Many of the men left wives and children behind and denied themselves of some of the comforts of life, but it would be the making of many younger members of the battalion and installed in their minds the principles of subordination and duty. They should be all the better for the sojourn, which may last twelve months.

The route taken was via St Owen's Street, High Town, Commercial Street, and Commercial Road, and cheers were frequently raised. Thousands of people followed the men to the station. But by a wise precaution on the part of the police, they could not gain admittance; if they had, the men would never have gotten away that night. As it was, a considerable section got on the platform, and several women rushed the police, but the railway officials were in no way hampered. Six men were allotted to every compartment so that they were not overcrowded, and the officers had the use of a saloon. There were altogether twelve coaches, two horse boxes containing five horses apiece, and two trucks with the usual baggage. The whole was drawn by a goods engine, which was timed to reach Reading at 8.40 p.m., when a South-Eastern engine would take on the load. Gravesend would probably not be reached until midnight. As the train moved out of the station, loud cheers were raised, and the band, which had taken up a position at the extreme end of the station, played "Auld Lang Syne". This was exactly at five o'clock, so there was fifteen-minute delay, but otherwise there was not a hitch in the arrangements.

Back in the Army Again, Sergeant.
Back in the army again,
Oo said I knew when the troopship was due,
I'm back in the army again.

—Rudyard Kipling

THE RAILWAY BLOCKHOUSES

The protect from destruction and sabotage the railway lines, and in particular bridges that connected Cape Town and other seaports to the interior, it was decided in early 1900 to construct a series of blockhouses that interconnected with each other along the railway system. These fortifications included many impressive stone structures that were costly and time-consuming to build. The Twenty-Third Field Company, Royal Engineers, based at Middlebury, Transvaal, was able to design a blockhouse that army units could construct themselves, and in early 1901 the first began to arrive in the Shropshire Light Infantry area.

They consisted of two skins of corrugated iron four and half inches apart, and the interior was filled with shingle. Loopholes were provided, and the whole was roofed in. They were cheap and required little transport; the usual garrison was a non-commissioned officer and six men.

The system was gradually increased, with a continuous barbed wire fence entanglement surrounding each blockhouse and a telephone line linking up the whole system. On 2 November 1901, orders were issued that a trench three feet deep and three feet wide was to be started so as to make a continues trench from blockhouse to blockhouse, as well as a barbed wire fence. The object of this was to prevent the Boers from crossing the railway line at night. At this of the year, it was very misty, especially around Belfast, which enabled the Boers to more easily cross. In some cases, the blockhouses were a considerable distance apart. Each man in the blockhouse had to work two and half hours daily digging this trench, in addition to his other duties. In this work, the men were engaged in erecting and occupying blockhouses towards Dalmanutha in one direction and towards Wonderfontein in the other.

By the end of the war, there were about six thousand miles of railway line and eight thousand Blockhouse manned by fifty thousand British troops.

**The twilight swallows the thicket,
The starlight reveals the ridge,
The whistle shills to the picket,
We are changing the guard at the bridge.**

—Rudyard Kipling

THE SECOND BATTALION OF THE WORCESTER REGIMENT

The Second Battalion sailed on the *Tintagel Castle* on 16 December 1899 and arrived at Cape Town on 6 January 1900. Along with the Second Bedfordshire, First Royal Irish Regiment, and Second Wiltshire, they formed the Twelfth Brigade under Major-General Clements. The brigade went to the Colesberg-Naauwpoort district upon arriving in the Cape Colony, and after General French and the bulk of his mounted troops were taken to Modder River for the Kimberley and Bloemfontein advances, General Clements was barely able to hold his own in the advanced and extended position he inherited. On 12 February 1900, the right flank of the British at Slingersfontein came under a strong attack by the Boers. The key position of the British at this point was a Kopje, held by three companies of the Second Battalion Worcester Regiment. The Boers made a fierce onslaught but were as fiercely repelled. The Boers do not favour night attacks, but they used darkness for taking up a good position and pushing onwards as soon as it was possible in the dawn's early light.

The Second Battalion of the Worcester Regiment contained no less than 450 marksmen in its ranks, and these companies upon the hill (later named Worcester Hill) were well provided with these veterans. Their fire was so accurate that the Boers were unable to advance any further. Throughout the long day, a desperate duel was maintained between the two lines of riflemen.

The commanding officer, Lieutenant-Colonel Charles Cuningham, and his second in command, Brevet-Major Major Kennedy Stubbs, were killed in this action, and the Bisley Champion of the battalion, with a bullet through his thigh, expended a hundred rounds before sinking from loss of blood. With the coming of darkness, the Boers withdrew with a loss of over two hundred killed or wounded. The battalion lost fifteen men killed, with three officers and thirty men wounded. On the fifteenth, the fighting was again severe, with the Worcesters losing two killed and two wounded and fourteen taken prisoner. The Wiltshires lost very heavily. In the operation for the surrounding of Prinsloo, the battalion took part but had only very slight loss.

When the brigade was broken up, the Second Battalion Worcester Regiment accompanied General Clements to the Megaliesberg, north-west of Pretoria. His troops at that time were the Second Northumberland Fusiliers, First Battalion Border Regiment, Second. Yorkshire Light Infantry, Sixth RFA, and nine hundred mounted infantries under Colonel Ridley. The column concentrated at Commando Nek and did much hard work under General Clements, and afterwards under General Cummingham and other commanders, in clearing and bringing under control the Rustenburg-Krugersdorp district. Clements reversed at Nooitgedacht on 13 December 1900.

In the second phase of the war, the battalion was employed in the north-east of the Orange River Colony, and for part of 1901, it held Heilbron and other points in the district. On 22 October 1904, the battalion embarked at Durban for Colombo and was stationed in Ceylon for two years.

THE MOUNTED INFANTRY

All battalions on arrival in South Africa had to provide a mounted infantry company. A company of mounted infantry consisted of 142 men formed into four troops of thirty-two men. The company was commanded by a major or captain, all were mounted, and each company had two wagons which carried baggage and food.

The order for one company to proceed to De Aar, where it would find horses and saddlery and thereupon would become a mounted infantry company, led to serious complications. Many of the men crossed a horse that day for the first time in their lives, and a mounted infantryman who could neither ride nor properly look after his horse did not offer much fighting value.

The mounted infantry companies were formed into eight mounted infantry battalions, and in April 1900 they formed two brigades. All were armed with infantry rifles and not the cavalry carbine. Two companies of mounted infantry were attached to each cavalry brigade, and these two mounted infantry companies amounted to 306 men, 310 horses, two machine runs, and nine wagons.

About the need for mounted infantry, General Roberts wrote on 27 April 1900,

> Before we can put an end to this war, there will have to be a number of changes in our present military system and tactics. Corps of mounted infantry must be raised, so say 200 or 300 strong and each have a district, not too large, and to live as much as possible on the country. Two or more guns to be given to each corps. All the infantry to garrison the towns and places of importance. Then and not till then will this brigandage cease and peace be established. We can go on till doomsday hunting these Boers with infantry, they only laugh at us.

From these official reports and records of the mounted infantry companies in South African Boer War, we gain no information regarding the conditions in which these mounted infantries had to endure. They in constant contact with the Boer commandos, who engaged in driving them farther away from their supply lines. This required them to be out in all weather, summer and winter, without cover. There was little chance of a wash once a week, or of a bath once in a month. They cooked their own meals and were on rations—often half rations or less. There were infrequent paydays, worn out uniforms and equipment, knockout horses, and only their knowledge and eyesight to understand the hazardous local conditions while they were tasked with locating and bringing pressure to the enemy.

HORSES IN THE BOER WAR

War Office records show that 400,346 horses, donkeys, and mules were "expended" during the course of the South African Boer War. Military horses of that time were divided into three classes: cavalry, mounted infantry, and gun horses. The role of the cavalry horse was the most demanding, and consequently they were the most expensive and of the best breeds. Gun horses came in two classes, the field battery horse and the royal horse artillery. The former was the draught style of animal, and the latter was a first-class carriage horse.

The mounted infantry (MI) did not require anything like the type of animal used by the cavalry or artillery. The mounted infantry man dismounted to fight and only used his horse as a means of locomotion, so a much less pretentious animal served him. The major sources for the army horses were the United Kingdom, Australia, Argentina, Hungary, and South Africa. The United Kingdom provided most of the cavalry and artillery horses because of the requirements for breed horses.

Australia provided horses known as Walers. The term *Waler* probably comes from the Indian army because the Hunter Valley in Australia provided many horses for the remount depots of India. When speaking of these horses, India officers called them Walers because of their New South Wales origin. From then on, this term was used to designate all Australian horses used by the British army regardless of place of birth. Argentina supplied many horses, but they were not well liked by the soldier. They were squat, short-legged cobs with big hips, bad shoulders, and very arched necks. The best thought of were the little ponies ridden by the Burma mounted infantry (recruited from units serving in Burma). These sturdy, small ponies were about thirteen hands high and were said to be able to carry a soldier and all his kit from dawn to dusk, day after day, on a diet of a few handfuls of mealies.

Cape ponies were said not to be worth the name of horse because they were small, weedy, narrow little things, but they were full of "quality". They were native to the country, did not become sick, and stood more work than any other style of horse. Basuto ponies were more solid, and hardships that laid low other horse were as nothing to a genuine Basuto. It should be remembered that it was on Cape ponies that the Boer did their work, and the rapidity of their movement showed that they were generally well mounted. However, they tended to travel with little food or equipment, and life was easier for their horses.

Only one soldier in the Seventh Mounted Infantry rode the same horse from February 1900 to June 1902: Corporal George Sutton and his Cape pony Kit were together for the whole trek. The mounted infantry operated in South Africa's Second Boer War for two years and eight months. They also had the job of burning all Boer farms, the slaughter of all farm animals, and the removal of women and children from the destroyed properties. Over 26,000 Boer prisoners of war were sent to camps overseas in Saint Helena, Ceylon, and Bermuda.

THE CALL-UP FOR VOLUNTEERS

It would seem that the turning point in the government's attitude regarding the use of volunteers in South Africa occurred during December 1899. In that month, the army experienced three major defeats within six days, known as the Black Week, resulting in serious public concern in Britain and a demand for changes in military command and tactics.

A special army order dated 2 January 1900 authorised the raising of a number of volunteer service companies by county regiments. Each company was to contain 116 men between the ages of twenty and thirty-five, and they were required to be first-class shots, physically fit, of good character, passed as efficient for the last two years, and preferably unmarried in order to overcome the legal restrictions of the Volunteer Act. The service period was for one year. The number of companies formed were to be for each regular battalion then servicing in South Africa. Upon arrival in South Africa, a company would be attached to its affiliated regiment and be under the orders of its commanding officer.

After reaching South Africa, the volunteer service companies joined their regiments and served alongside their comrades in the regular forces. The history of their service is that of their parent regiment.

With their service completed, the first series of volunteer companies were ordered home, their places taken by a newly formed group which had been raised under an army order issued in January 1901. These in turn came home after seeing a great deal of action and were again replaced by a fresh draft in 1902.

THE HEREFORDSHIRE CONTINGENT OF VOLUNTEERS FOR SOUTH AFRICA

On Tuesday, 16 January 1900, thirty-eight men from the Herefordshire Volunteer Rifle Corps departed Hereford railway station to travel to Shrewsbury and join the Shropshire Light Infantry, Volunteer Service Company. The Herefordshire contingent was composed of one lieutenant, two sergeants, one corporal, one bugler, and thirty-three men. They were sent to the following companies

A Company (Hereford): five
H Company (Hereford): four
B company (Ross): twenty, and one lieutenant
C company (Ledbury): three
D company (Bromyard): one
G company (Kingston): five

These men left Hereford wearing their corps scarlet uniform. The First Volunteer Service Company departed on 3 March 1900 on board the *Ninevah* and arrived with the Second Battalion, King's Shropshire Light Infantry on 2 May 1900.

NEWSPAPER EXCERPTS: THE YEOMANRY

The Shropshire company of the Imperial Yeomanry, 150 strong, under the command of Captain Gordon Wood, was inspected at Shrewsbury, on Wednesday by Lieutenant-Colonel F. C. Mayrick, who is appointed to command the first of the Imperial Yeomanry companies.

Colonel Mayrick expressed himself much gratified with the smart way the men drilled and hoped arrangements would be completed to enable them to embark for the front on the 27th, inst. Letters received in Hereford this week pointed to the fact that some of the men might sail on Sunday or Monday, but we believe later communications postpone the date to the end of the month."

The Yeomanry whilst in South Africa did not perform their duties as efficacious as the mounted infantry. The Boers captured all the Irish Yeomanry horses at one time, and it was the same commando that rushed the Yeomanry at Lindley. One report states that their commanding officer got rather wild with them each time they were on Flank-Guard 2 or 3 would get captured, and get sent back stripped with only a shirt and a note re good equipment but poor horses.

—*Hereford Journal*, Saturday, 20 January 1900

The Hereford Militia, officially known as the 4th. Battalion King's Shropshire Light Infantry, returned on Thursday 1st. November 1900 to their headquarters at Hereford for disbandment, after having been on garrison duty for over a year. It will be remembered that the Militia were called up for duty last November and left our ancient city one dreary, wintery day of fog in the air and snow under-foot. For Gravesend, where under the popular command of Colonel Scudamore Lucas, they were quartered for some time, and at a later period moved to Ireland. The battalion during its embodiment, 182 men had volunteered for service at the front, and have been or still were serving in South Africa.

—*Hereford Journal*, Saturday, 3 November 1900

The departure from Shrewsbury of the Shropshire Volunteer Service Company. After undergoing a strict course of training at Shrewsbury for several weeks, the Volunteer Service Company formed by the 1st and 2nd Shropshire and 1st Herefordshire Volunteer Battalions will leave Shrewsbury early to-morrow (Saturday Morning) and proceed to Liverpool, where they will embark on board the "Seavic" for South Africa.

—*Shrewsbury Chronicle*, Friday, 22 March 1901

The Visit to Hereford by Princess Beatrice of Battenberg: The Presentation of Medals in High Town, Tuesday, 13 May 1902

The military ceremony in High Town during the afternoon was the popular feature of the day's proceedings and attracted an enormous concourse. The volunteers, headed by their band, marched into the square around two o'clock, and the permanent staff of the Fourth Battalion, KSLI with the men who had been to the front with the Second Shropshires, under the command of Captain Symonds-Taylor, arrived about the same time. The turnout was very smart.

The volunteers lined the greater portion of High Town, St Peter's Street to beyond the site of the municipal building. The weather during the wait that followed was not very cheering. There was a cold wind, and the rain seemed to threaten several times, but happily it did not fall. Occasionally, as if to make amends for these inconveniences, the sun shone forth brightly, but never for long. The scene was a remarkable one. Pavements and roadways were crowded, and windows and roofs of practically all the houses in the neighbourhood were filled with people. From these vantage points, the scene must have been striking. The crowds stretched in either direction on the line of route as far as the eye could see.

The route was kept open by a number of mounted policemen, who had a difficult task to perform. The crowd, as a holiday crowd always is, was humorous, and the time was beguiled by many little pleasantries. Several of the volunteers came in for a great deal of good-natured chaff, and the advent of a dog into the carefully kept arena was signal for a loud burst of hooting and laughter. The mounted policemen did not escape the criticism of the crowd by any means. More than once, as a member of the force backed his horse against the people to send them farther away, his horse was seen to bound quickly into the open again, the horse's tail having been pulled by a bystander; the animal and policeman on its back bobbed up and down as the crowd roared. The police also entered into the spirit of the thing and heartily laughed at the various amusing incidents that occurred. The time passed very slowly, and it was not until several minutes after three o'clock that the signal was given that Her Royal Highness and party were approaching. The princess drove with Lord and Lady Chesterfield from the palace via Broad Street, and she was accompanied by the travelling escort of yeomanry. Several carriages followed, among these the bishop, and the dean of the mounted policemen brought up the rear.

As the royal party arrived in High Town, hearty cheers were raised, and the band played the national anthem. Colonel Robinson, commanding the Fifty-Third Regiment District and representing General Swayne, commander of the North-Western District, was in command of the military parade. Colonel Lucas-Scudamore commanded the Herefordshire Militia, and Colonel Scobie commanded the Herefordshire Volunteers. Also present was Colonel Robinson to receive the princess. The distribution of the military decorations took place immediately. Colonel Robinson handed the Distinguished Conduct Medals to Her Royal Highness, Colonel Lucas-Scudamore handed the military medal, Colonel Scobie handed the volunteer clasps, and Surgeon Captain Thompson handed the Bearer Company medals.

The first to receive their medals were Corporal Panners, DCM, late of the Shropshire Imperial Yeomanry. The decorations were pinned on the men's breasts by the princess amid ringing cheers. Several militia men were next to receive their medals, and the clasps were distributed to the service men of the volunteers, among them being Lieutenant Cutler, of Ross. Major Rankin, who was mounted on a splendid Arab horse, also came forward, leading his steed by the reins, and he received a medal and three clasps for his service with Rimington's Guides. The last to receive their medals were the men of Bearer Company.

The recipients of decorations, besides those already specially mentioned above, were as follows.

Herefordshire Volunteer Service Company

Colour Sgt. Lewis, Sgt. Griffin, Sgt. Badham, Corp. Dalby, L/Corp. Morgan, and Privates Beavan, Bethell, Brookes, Fisher, Corfield, Cox, C. Davies, E. Davies, Drew, England, Evans, Farmer, George, Godsell, Groves, Hayward, Howls, Jenkins, Lewis, O'Niell, Palfrey, Powell, J. Price, S. Price, Pyart, Small, A. Taylor, M. Taylor, Williams, Wyine. Privates Palamountain, and Rushgrove received long service medals.

Welsh Border Brigade Bearer Company

Medal and three clasps: Private C. Davies
Medal and two clasps: Corporal H. Griffiths
Medal: Private W. E. Hill, Corporal A. J. G. Inns, Private J. Leeks, Lance Corporal N. Moddy, Lance Corpl. H. J. Naish, Private G. Niblett, Private J. Niblett, Corporal J. Ough, Private R. J. Probert, Private W. Verrill, Sgt. E. J. Warwick, Private J. Webber.
Lance-Corporal C. M. E. Vaugham and Private A. E. Smith were deceased, so the medals were sent to their respective relations—a somewhat unique position for as small a force as the Hereford
Corporal N. Griffiths and Private J. Webber had both returned to the front, so their medals would be sent to their friends.

The reason the other men besides the first two named did not have their clasps was that the clasp rolls were not forwarded from South Africa. What would prove a one was that seven different bars would be worn by various members of the service. One acting warrant officer thirteen non-commissioned officers and men who served with the Rhodesian field force had already received their medals in London at the hands of the director general of the Army Medical Service.

THE RETURN OF THE HEREFORD VOLUNTEERS

The following appeared in the *Hereford Journal* on Saturday, 7 June 1902.

The Hereford men forming part of the 2nd Volunteer Service Company will arrive at Barr's Court station this (Friday) evening at 7.40; there's every reason to believe that a popular demonstration awaits them. The men travelled from the Cape on the transport Lake Erie, which arrived at Southampton on Wednesday. The Shropshire company to which the Herefordshire men belong, consists of two officers (Lieut. Anthony being one) and 95 men, and their fellow voyagers included men from various regiments. The troops did not hear of the conclusion of peace until the pilot boarded the vessel in the Solent, There upon they cheered lustily, and were in high spirits when they came into port, and the scene of Southampton was most enthusiastic.

The Shropshire company proceeded to Shrewsbury on Thursday, where they were met with an enthusiastic reception, being publicly welcomed by the Mayor and Corporation entertaining them to luncheon whilst this (Friday) afternoon it had been arranged that they should receive their South African medals at the hands of Colonel Robinson in the agricultural show yard in the town. The Hereford men will afterwards proceed home. The Ross contingent will go straight through to Ross a little in advance of the journey of the city men, being expected home about seven o'clock. The Herefordians who number eight, the ninth, Private Carless, being at Netley Hospital, will as we have intimated reach Barr's Court at 7.40. They will be met at the station by the headquarters company and the battalion band, and march through the centre of the city to the Drill Hall. It is hoped that the flags will be everywhere displayed, and the citizens scarcely need to asked to turn out and give the men a hearty welcome.

On Saturday night the Mayor (Alderman Symonds) will entertain them, together with those members of the Militia, Yeomanry and Volunteers whose service have not yet been publicly recognised, to supper at the Drill Hall, where a large company is expected. Each man of B Company will receive a silver watch and an illuminated address and will entertained at a public dinner at Ross.

The names of the returning men are: Lieutenant Percy Anthony, Private W. Williams, Private H. Lee, Private J. Grady, Private C. Hull, Private A. Williams, Private J. Norton, Bugler F. C. Edwards.

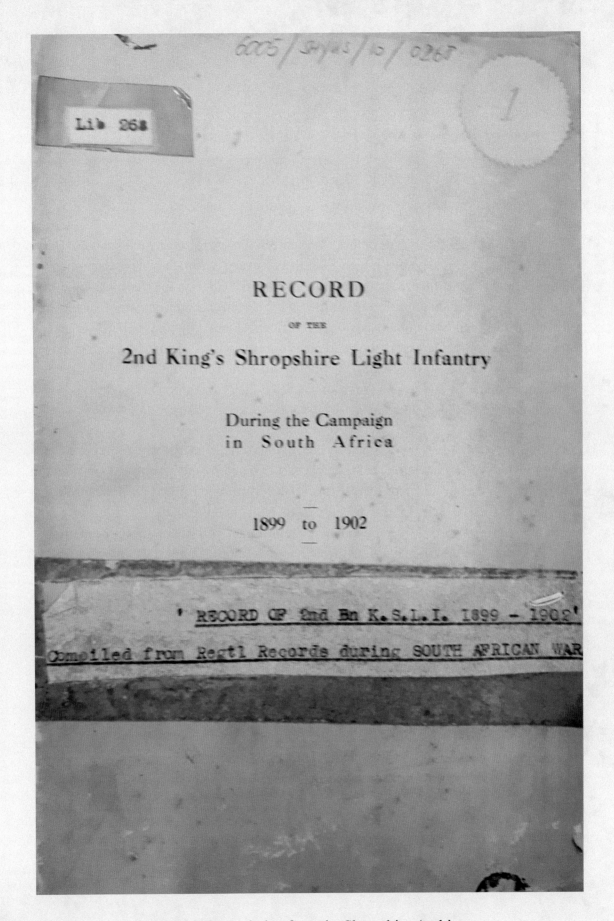

With kind permission from the Shropshire Archive.

THE KING'S SHROPSHIRE LIGHT INFANTRY

After the call-up of the reservists, the Second Battalion, under the command of Colonel J. Spens, sailed for South Africa on 7 November 1899 with 29 officers and 752 men. They went on the hired transport ship *Arawa* from Southampton, and on 10 November, the *Arawa* put back to Southampton due to electrical problems. It reached Las Palmas on 15 November and arrived Cape Town on 1 December 1899. After their arrival, they were mainly employed on the lines of communication in Western Cape Colony for about two months, with the headquarters being at Orange River Station. They served with the detachment at Zoutpans Drift before advancing into the Free State. It was part of the Nineteenth Brigade under the command of General Smith-Dorrien.

On 21 December 1899 at 4.35 p.m., The *Jelunga* sailed from Empress Dock, Southampton, with 30 officers and 1,302 men on board, including the Second Shropshire Light Infantry, under Lt. English and 2/Lt. Delme-Murray, and 175 men. The *Jelunga* left Gibraltar on 28 December for South Africa.

The 2nd Battalion King's Shropshire Light Infantry BEFORE DEPARTURE to South Africa.

SECOND BATTALION KING'S SHROPSHIRE LIGHT INFANTRY: REGIMENTAL RECORDS KEPT DURING THE WAR

Courtesy of Soldiers of Shropshire Museum.

The following passages come direct from the regimental records, taken from November 1899 to 6 May 1902.

November 1899, On the 7th November 1899, the Battalion left Aldershot to take part in the South African Campaign, being detailed for lines of communication duties. The establishment was as follows; 29 officers and 990 non-commissioned officers and men. 26 officers and 757 non-commissioned officers and men embarked at Southampton on the SS *Arawa* on the 7th November, the remainder proceeding via East India Docks, London, on SS *Chicago*. After a pleasant voyage, on which various physical exercises took place, the SS *Arawa* arrived at Cape Town on December 1st, to find the SS *Chicago* awaiting them. Orders were issued to disembark next day, to proceed to Naauwport by train. But on arrival at De Arr Junction the destination was changed to Orange River, the Regiment arriving at the Camp there on the 4th December.

The journey from Cape Town to Orange River Station took 4 days, and the train stopped periodically for the Battalion to cook its meals, and at times when the train went slowly up steep hills the men were able to get out and stretch their legs.

December 5th. Outpost lines were this day taken up by the Battalion, three and a half Companies being detailed for duty, of which two Companies were stationed at Orange River Bridge.

December 7th. Sergeant Mickleburgh and Private Taylor were this day shot whilst on outpost duty, being mistaken for Boers.

December 25th. Xmas Day, The Battalion attended Divine Service this morning and all fatigues were discontinued for the day. A pint of beer was issued from the Canteen funds. The following message was received from Her Majesty the Queen by the Commander-in-Chief: "I wish you and all my brave soldiers a happy Xmas. God protect and bless you all. V.R.I."

December 29th. Inspected by Major-General Elliott Wood, C.B.

January 6th. 1900. A, B, and C Companies under Lieut-Colonel J. Spens, proceeded to Zoutpans Drift for duty, thereby being the first British Troops to occupy the Orange Free State. No opposition was encountered on the march.

January 17th. Headquarters returned to Orange River. Major Bulman assumed command at Zoutpans Drift.

January 20th. A draft of 150 non-commissioned officers and men under Lieutenant English and 2nd. Lieut. Delme-Murray joined the Battalion from England. This day a Regimental Boxing Tournament was held, when some interesting bouts took place, but unfortunately, owing to movement of Troops it could not be finished. The Battalion at this time was heavily pressed by having to furnish large fatigue parties at the Army Service Corps. Depot and on the railway for construction of new lines.

January 24th. Instructions were received for the Battalion to furnish 103 specially selected men to form a Mounted Infantry Company. D Company provided the most, officers being Capt. J. J. White, Lieut. H. M. Smith, 2/Lieut. F. Fitzgerald, and 2/Lieut. J. C. Hooper. On February 9th 2/Lieut. E. A. Underwood and 28 NCOs and men were included. The 85th Company left Orange River for De Aar, where horses and equipment were to be drawn on. Here the 85th was joined by other new companies from the Royal Warwickshire Regiment, the Yorkshire Regiment, and the Duke of Cornwall's Light Infantry. And thus constituted, it went through the war as an element of the 4th Regiment of Mounted Infantry. Lt. Col. St. G. C. Henry of the Northumberland Fusiliers was appointed Commanding Officer.

February 9th. It was officially notified that the Battalion would shortly be ordered to the front, to form part of the 19th Brigade under Brigadier-General Smith Dorrien D.S.O. The news gave universal satisfaction after our long stay at Orange River.

February 11th. Four Companies proceeded by train to Graspan being followed next day by the Companies at Zoutpans Drift. The 19th Brigade now consisted of the Gordon Highlanders, Canadian Royal Infantry, Duke of Cornwall's Light Infantry, and our Battalion. Lieut. E. P. Dorrien Smith was appointed acting Aide-de-Camp to the Brigadier-General (his uncle).

February 13th. The Brigade marched to Ramadam to join a Column being formed there under the Field Marshal Lord Roberts.

February 14th. Marched to Reit River, A very hot and trying march to the Troops, water being very scarce. Distance 16 miles.

February 15th. A party of sick, unable to perform forced marches, was left at Reit River prior to the departure of the Column for Jacobsdal. Arrived this day at Wegdraai, near Jacobsdal.

February 16th. Marched to Jacobsdal, where information was received of Cronje's flight from Magersfontein. Orders were received to follow with the idea of stopping his flight to Bloemfontein. Orders were received to march next morning at 2.50 a.m., these being subsequently countermanded, and we left Jacobsdal just after dusk, forming the rear guard of the Brigade. Marching was continued all night, and Klip Drift was reached at daybreak, Two companies left this day for Modder River as escort to a Telegraph Company, Royal Engineers.

February 17th. Rested during the day, and marched again in the evening towards Paardeberg, arriving there about 5.30 a.m., on the 18th. February and found that Cronje and his Army were holding a strong position in the bed of the Modder ("Muddy") River.

February 18th. (Sunday) After a short rest the Brigade was ordered into action. F and H Companies taking up a position on the south bank of the river, A, E, and G Companies waded the river, breast deep, by sections of fours, the current of the river being very strong. A very long day was experienced under a hot fire, which was maintained without cessation until dark. The losses of the Battalion this day (although always in the firing line) were 4 officers 8 NCO's and men killed and 4 officers and 32 NCO's and men wounded.

February 19th. Practically a postponement of hostilities the Boer's being entirely hemmed in on all sides. Towards evening trenches were dug, which the Battalion (now reinforced by B and C Companies from Modder River) occupied during the night, advancing next day nearer the enemy's laager.

February 20th. The Battalion occupied the advanced trenches from this date until relieved by the Gordon Highlanders on the 22nd. During our occupation of the trenches desultory fire was kept up on both sides, the Boers principally sniping, our men returning the fire whenever opuntias occurred. Our losses during these three days were 5 men wounded one man eventually dying of his wounds.

February 22nd. Relieved by the Gordons and bivouacked by the Drift to rest. The same day, however, heavy rain set in, and there were rumours of De Wet, trying to reinforce Cronje, so the Battalion was ordered out on outpost duty, remaining out until relieved by the Cornwell L. Infantry.

February 26th. The Brigade made an attack on the Boer laager in the night (the laager was now almost destroyed by shell fire), firing long range volleys to cover the more direct advance of the Royal Canadians. Lieutenant Atchison was severely wounded on the morning of the 27th, just before the order was received that Cronje had surrendered. Thus, ended a siege that had lasted ten days.

February 27th. The Brigade advanced and bivouacked near the Boer Laager, and after the prisoners had been removed was engaged clearing all debris, filth, etc.

A report on the battle records the following. Smith-Dorrien was with the forward troops all through the battle. The Boers in the laager were surrounded, and Kitchener thought that it could be captured in a day. He was wrong. The Boers were extremely well protected by their clever camouflage and well-designed group of trenches, which also contained wives and families living a strange sort of troglodytic existence. The battle lasted from 18 to 27 February 1900. Inside the laager the Boers were in a bad way. They had casualties, had lost most of the horses, and were no longer mobile. There were dead animals, screaming children, and a terrible stench. Four thousand Boers eventually surrendered, including 50 women and 150 wounded. British casualties totalled 24 officers and 279 NCOs and men killed. Fifty-nine officers and 847 NCOs and men wounded.

Smith-Dorrien and his staff rode in advance with a white flag to organize the surrender. The Boer trenches were marvellous, narrow at the top and so deep that only a man's head and shoulders were visible standing upright. They must have been practically shell-proof, and were situated in extraordinary little odd corners and placed along the river for miles, as well as in the big trenches outside the laager.

February 28th. Brigade Order No. 3 of this date was published. "Lord Roberts has received the following telegram, dated 27th inst., from the Secretary of State for War: Her Majesty's Government sincerely congratulate you and the Force under your Command on your great and opportune achievement, It is published for information. The Field Marshal Commanding-in-Chief desires to express to all Troops under his Command his high appreciation of their conduct during the recent operations, by the endurance they have shown through long and trying marches, and the gallantry they have displayed when engaged with the enemy, that they worthily upheld the tradition of Her Majesty's Army. He has every reason to reply on the spirit and resolution of British soldiers, and he confidently trusts to their devotion to their Queen and Country to bring to a successful close the operations so auspiciously begun."

March 3rd. Owing to the insanitary conditions of the laager and the surroundings of the Paardeburg the Troops moved to Osfontein, remaining there until 7th March.

March 7th. The Brigade proceeded to Poplar Grove, the Battalion executing a brilliant march of twenty miles, attacking the enemy by a flank movement, and capturing a gun. An awfully bad night was experienced here, as the transport did not arrive until the early hours of the morning, so we had to go without our blankets and food. One man was wounded.

Brigade Order No 3 of this date was published. The Major General Commanding the Brigade wishes all ranks of the Brigade he has the honour to Command to understand how thoroughly he appreciates the spirited zeal shown by them since the Brigade assembled at Graspan on 12th February. All have been called on for extraordinary exertions and have had to undergo forced marches, short rations, frequent wettings, want of water and sleep, and also severe and trying fighting, concluding with an extremely arduous flank march yesterday of some twenty miles. It will be gratifying for them to know that yesterday's march turned the Boer position, threaten their rear, and causing them to retreat in haste, making then cease fire on our naval guns and abandon their own gun (which the Shropshire L.I. captured) It also enabled the Highland Brigade to advance direct on the enemy's trenches without opposition, and further caused the retirement of a large number of mounted men, which had held out Mounted Infantry (on the left flank of the Brigade) in check throughout the morning. It will be gratifying to all to know that thanks to the untiring energy shown by everyone the 19th Brigade has established a high name for itself, which the Major-General feels confident all will continue to do their utmost to maintain. He regrets the Brigade has suffered the loss of so many brave officers and men, and especially Lieut. Col. Aldworth of the Cornwell L.I. The Brigade crossed to the south bank of the Modder River without mishap. The Major-General, remarking on this occurrence, stating, judging by the time it took previous Units to cross the Modder, it was judged that it would take the 19th Brigade eight hours, but thanks, however, to the officers in charge of fatigue parties, and the energy in which the men worked, it was completed in three hours. The Battalion now formed part of the centre Column of 3, under Lord Roberts, advancing on to Bloemfontein, which was reached on the 14th March. The 19th Brigade bivouacked at Ferriera Siding this day, and marched near to the town next day. Not much opposition had been met with during the advance from Poplar Grove, but forced marches on reduced rations were regularly experienced. The Brigade marched to Bloemfontein, and encamped at the Rifle Range, but without tents.

March 18th. The following Army Order was published this day. "It affords the Field Marshal Commanding-in-Chief the greatest pleasure in congratulating the Army in South Africa on various events that have occurred during the past few weeks, and he would especially offer his sincere thanks to that portion of the Army which, under his immediate Command have taken part in the operations resulting yesterday in the capture of Bloemfontein. On the 12th inst. His Force crossed the boundary which divided the Orange Free State from British Territory. Three days later Kimberley was relieved. On the 15th day the bulk of the Boer Army in this State under one of their most trusted Generals was taken prisoners. On the 17th. day news was received that Ladysmith was relieved, and on the 13th. March 29 days from the commencement of operations, the Capital of the Orange Free State was occupied. This is a record of which any Army might well be proud; a record which could not have been achieved except by earnest well-disciplined men determined to do their duty, and to surmount whatever difficulties or dangers might be encountered. Exposed to extreme heat by day, bivouacking under heavy rains, marching long distances (not infrequently with reduced rations) the endurance cheerfulness, and gallantry displayed by all ranks are beyond praise, and Lord Roberts feels sure that neither H.M. the Queen nor the British Nation will be unmindful of the efforts made by this Force to uphold the honour of their Country. The Field Marshal desires specially to refer to the fortitude and heroic spirit with which the wounded have borne their suffering. Owing to the great extent of country over which modern battles have to be fought, it is not always. Possible to afford immediate aid to those that are struck down. Many hours had, indeed at times elapsed before some of the wounded could be attended to, but not a murmur, or word of complaint had been uttered.

"The anxiety was that their wounded comrades might be attended to first. In assuring every officer and man how much he appreciates their efforts in the past, Lord Roberts is confident that in the future they will continue to show the same resolution and soldierly qualities, and to lay down their lives if need be (as so many brave men have already done) in order to ensure that the war in South Africa may be brought to a satisfactory conclusion."

March 20th. Major Doyle joined the Battalion this day for duty. Sergeant Meredith was granted a commission in Her Majesty's Army for good service in the field.

March 21st. The Brigade was inspected this day by Lieut.-General Sir. H. Colville, Commanding 9th Division, who made a careful inspection of each man. A march past ended the inspection, in connection with which the following order was published by the General Officer Commanding: "The G.O.C., of the Brigade notifies that it was very gratifying to him after parade this morning to be congratulated by the Lieut.-General Commanding the Division on the excellence of the turn out of the Brigade, and smartness under arms. Every man was doing his best, and the march past was the best the Major General had seen for years, and he spent his last years (before coming to South Africa in Malta. where Ceremonial parades abound."

March 30th. The Battalion paraded for medical inspection by the Principal Medical Officer, with the view of picking out all men considered unable to march.

March 31st. Paraded at 5.20 a.m. and marched in Brigade to Waterval Drift (about 20 miles) with the object of assisting General Broadwood's Cavalry Brigade, which was hard pressed at Samma's Post. Unfortunately, we did not arrive in time, but succeeded in supporting General Porter's Cavalry Brigade on the 1st April thereby contributing largely to the recapture of 87 of our prisoners from the Boers.

April 2nd. A serious accident occurred this morning through the careless handling of a loaded rifle, which resulted in four men being wounded.

April 3rd. The Battalion returned to Bloemfontein.

April 4th. The Brigade was again suddenly ordered out this day to Reitfontein and Leewkop to prevent, if possible a projected conference of Boer Generals at the latter place on the 5th inst. However, the Boers obtained news of our move, and we only succeeded in shelling and driving off some 200 of them.

April 6th. Brigade returned to Bloemfontein.

April 14th. Lieutenant Smith invalided to England.

April 17th. A draft of 100 NCOs and men joined from England.

April 21st. The Brigade left Bloemfontein presumably for a three day's reconnaissance in the direction of the Waterworks and encamped in tents of the 18th Brigade at Springfield, until the 24th April.

April 24th. Left Mamema at 5 a.m. to march to Thala N'Chu, but came in contact with a force of Boers at Israel's Poort, which was eventually driven back. The Battalion encamped close to the scene of the engagement. Our losses were one man killed and one man wounded.

April 30th. The Brigade marched at 5 a.m. and quickly came into action at Hout Nek near Thala N'Chu, were a stubborn fight lasting two days ensued. The enemy had guns and pom-poms, and repeatedly shelled the baggage Column and the hospital, without however doing much damage. Our Battalion's losses this day were 1 killed and 5 wounded.

May 1st. The fighting was resumed at daybreak, although indications were not wanting that the Boers had moved the majority of their laager during the previous night. One half of B Company, under Colour Sergeant Scous, managed to seize a position, and although subjected to a severe cross fire (which caused in this small party 10 casualties out of 40), maintained themselves stubbornly for four hours. Towards noon the other half of B Company and E Company took part in a bayonet charge with a party of Gordon Highlanders and Canadians and cleared the enemy from their position. Our losses this day were 12 NCOs and men of whom 3 died from their wounds.

May 2nd. A draft of 100 men under Captain Radcliffe, and the Volunteer Company, consisting of 113 NCOs and men, under Captain Trow, joined the Battalion this day, being heartily welcomed. The Brigade was now ordered to form part of the Winburg Column under Lieutenant-General Ian Hamilton the 21st Brigade being the other Infantry Brigade. The Column was on the right of the main advance to Johannesburg until the 25th May.

May 3rd. Marched to Jacobsrust, meeting with but slight opposition at the Vet River; bivouacked there and eventually reached Winburg on 5th May. The loyal inhabitants received the column very warmly and in many instances, men were given tea and coffee.

May 6th. Another medical inspection was held this day, and some 100 men were left behind in charge of Captain J. G. Forbes. The Column moved at 3 p.m., marching towards Kroonstad, and arriving at Dankbaarsfontein the same evening, where it remained until 9th May.

May 9th. Marched to Boomplaats.

May 10th. The Column came into action at Zand River, where the enemy was in strong force, but our Battalion was not seriously engaged, although subjected to a severe shell fire. We had no casualties. Crossed the river, and bivouacked 6 miles from it.

May 13th. Arrived at Kroonspruit about 5 miles from Kroonstad, where the Column remained until ordered to march east to Lindley on the 15th May.

May 17th. Crossed the Valsche River without opposition. The 21st Brigade left us here to proceed to Lindley.

May 19th. The 19th Brigade re-crossed the Valsch River and marched towards Heilbron, and captured the town on the 22nd May, with slight opposition on the way.

May 23rd. Left Heilbron, marching towards Prospect.

May 24th. Arrived at Prospect and came in touch with Lord Roberts Column of mounted men, advancing up to the railway. Her Majesty's birthday was celebrated this day. An extra issue of rum was given to the Troops, who gathered round the campfires and sang the National Anthem.

May 25th. Left Prospect and halted a couple of miles away to enable Lord Roberts Column to pass. We now formed the left Column of the advance to Johannesburg, a great strategic movement of Lord Roberts. After halting all day, the Battalion was detailed to escort a Convoy, and consequently was marching all night, only arriving in Camp in time to secure two hours rest previous to marching again at 6 a.m. towards the Vaal River.

May 26th. 40 NCOs and men of the 4th Battalion K.S.L.I. Stationed at Tipperary, Ireland, transferred to the 2nd Battalion K.S.L.I. for service in South Africa. The *Aurana* departed Queenstown 9th June 1900 for South Africa with 1 Officer and 100 Light Infantry men for the 2/Shropshires [Sgt. No. 1250, Francis Morris, my granddad, included].

May 27th. Marched to and crossed the Vaal River at Boschbank Drift, the Volunteer Company having the honour of being the first of the Battalion to cross.

May 28th. Marched to and encamped at Syferfontein. The Brigade was now marching on reduced rations, barely half-rations being issued, and which continued until the fall of Johannesburg, part biscuits, and mealie flour being issued.

May 28th. An attack was made on Johannesburg, the brunt of the fighting taking place at Doornkop, where Colonel J. Spens commanded the Infantry Division. This day the Battalion was rear guard, and did not come into action. The attack was first commenced by an attack by General French's mounted Troops, on the slopes of the Klipriversberg, the remainder of the Boers position was difficult to distinguish, also where their main body lay, but it was evident they occupied many miles of frontage, and some 3,500 to 4,000 yards from the Infantry all the grass was burnt. General Ian Hamilton after carefully reconnoitring the enemy's position decided that the Boers must be forced back, and the direct road to Florida opened, chiefly on account of the Division having no supplies. This was accordingly carried out by the 19th and 21st Brigades which worked splendidly, and by dusk the enemy had been driven out of every position in the field. Thus, ended a hard day's work, an 18-mile march, with four hours hard fighting. The Gordon Highlanders behaved splendidly during the fight, their losses being very heavy. The Battalion meanwhile escorting the baggage etc. had lost touch with the Division, mainly through following the Cavalry Brigade, and after aimlessly marching about for some hours, bivouacked close to a farm, being unable to locate the position of the Brigade. We marched early next morning, without food, towards Florida, and were met by a mounted orderly, who directed us to bivouac at that place. After arriving at our camping place, General Ian Hamilton rode up and said how pleased he was to see the Regiment had turned up again, as he had given us up for lost. A very pretty camping ground and all along the reefs signs of industry and commerce were to be seen, a network of telegraph and telephone wires run overhead. The Troops had now eaten their last days ration, and the only food obtainable was mealie meal. Part of a letter received from Lord Roberts by Genera Ian Hamilton was published in Orders this day: "I am delighted at your repeated success and grieved beyond measure at your poor Troops being without their proper food. A train full shall go to you today. I expect to get notice that Johannesbury surrenders this morning, and we shall then march on the town. I wish your Column, which has done so much to gain possession of it could be with us." However, the rations mentioned did not arrive, and we had to manage the best possible way under the circumstances, but a little mealie flour was issued (which the Troops mixed with water, and baked over a wood fire), which was not very appetizing.

June 2nd. Battalion moved Camp to Braamfontein on the north side of Johannesburg, and a percentage of men was allowed on pass into the town. All who could avail themselves of the opportunity did so, and small parties of men could be seen struggling back to Camp loaded with all supplies it was possible to get. Bread was obtainable in fairly large quantities.

June 3rd. The advance on Pretoria was resumed, our Force forming part of the centre Column. A long march unopposed by the enemy, and the next day at dawn we marched nearer the main Column. The 19th Brigade occupied a line of heights in support of the Mounted Infantry. These Heights were very steep, and only one gun and a pom-pom could, by great exertion be brought into action. Towards four o'clock firing practically ceased, and the action, in which the whole Army Corps had been engaged ceased.

June 5th. A memorable day, witnessing the surrender of Pretoria. Our Forces marched around to the western side of the town, and after passing through a narrow cleft in the walls of mountains, the town lay before us, looking very peaceful and picturesque, with red and blue roofs, the Government buildings being most conspicuous. At 2 p.m. Lord Roberts and his Staff entered the town, and proceeded to the Market Square, in which the largest buildings are situated, and the British Flag was hoisted over the Parliament House, amid deafening cheers. The victorious Troops (with the exception of a portion of Mounted Troops which occupied the surrounding hills) marched pass Lord Roberts in the Market Square, The 19th had the honour of being the first Troops to march past. The parade lasted three hours. As the Battalion marched past Lord Roberts with bayonets fixed, he remarked to Major-General Smith Dorrian, "I am given to understand that this is a very fine Regiment." To which Smith Dorrian replied, "It is, Sir, one of the finest in the Service." We then marched around the town and back to camp, so ending one of the most brilliant marches known in British annals, and all ranks were delighted that the goal of their ambition had at last been reached, after so many hardships, long marches, etc., having been experienced. The strength of the Battalion was now 20 officers and 680 NCOs and men. The following Order published by Lord Roberts, Commander-in-Chief, was promulgated to the Army in South Africa, 27th June, 1900: "In congratulating the British Army in South Africa on the occupation of Johannesburg and Pretoria, the one being the principal town, the other the Capital of the Transvaal, and also the relief of Mafeking, after an heroic defense of over 200 days, the Field Marshal Commander-in-Chief desires to place on record his appreciation of the gallantry and endurance displayed by the Troops, both those who have been employed in the less arduous duty of protecting the lines of communication through the Orange Free State. After the Force reached Bloemfontein on 13th March it was necessary to holt there for a certain period, through railway communication having been restored with Cape Colony, before supplies and necessaries of all kinds could be got up from the base. The rapid advance from the Modder River and the want of forage en route had told heavily on the horses of the Cavalry, Artillery, Mounted Infantry, and the

Transport mules and oxen, and to replace the casualties a considerable number of animals had to be provided. Throughout this six weeks the Army remained halted at Bloemfontein the enemy showed considerable activity, especially in the south eastern portion of the Orange Free State, but by the beginning of May everything was in readiness for a further advance into the enemy's country, and on the 2nd of that month active operations were again commenced. On the 12th Kroonstad, where Steyn had established the so-called Government of the Orange Free State was entered. On the 17th Mafeking was relieved, on the 31st Johnannesburg was occupied and on the 5th June, the British Flag waved over Pretoria.

"During the 35 days the Main Body of the forces marched over 300 miles including 15 days halt and engaged the enemy on six different occasions. The column under General Ian Hamilton's Column marched over 400 miles, including 10 days halt and was engaged with the enemy 28 times (the Battalion formed part of General Ian Hamilton's Column). During the recent operations the sudden variation in temperature between the warm sun in the day time and the bitter cold at night, have been peculiarly trying to the Troops, and owing to the necessary for rapid movements, the soldiers frequently had to bivouac after long and trying marches without blankets and firewood, and with scanty rations. The cheerful spirit with which difficulties have been overcome, and hardships disregarded, are deserving of the highest praise, and in thanking all ranks for their successful efforts to obtain the object in view, Lord Roberts is proud to think that the soldiers under his Command have worthily upheld the traditions of Her Majesty's Army in fighting in marching, and in the admirable discipline which has been maintained through a period of no ordinary trial and difficulty."

June 6th. Major General Smith Dorrien, Commanding 19th Brigade on addressing the Battalion at Pretoria, on June 6th, said: "Colonel Spens, officers and men of the King's Shropshire Light Infantry. I had no intention of speaking to you this morning, but after giving me such a hearty welcome, I feel I must say something. I first time I saw you under fire was at Paardeburg, and I was much struck at the magnificent way in which the leading Companies opened out for the attack, which at once showed me you thoroughly understood the art of skirmishing. The next was at Poplar Grove, and I asked Colonel Spens if he could advance and take up a certain position. This was over an open piece of ground, commanded on both sides by kopjes occupied by Boers with guns. This required a great deal of dash and determination, but it was done. The Boers were driven out and a gun captured by you and whenever we met the enemy, and I know the Shropshires were in front, I was confident of success. You are now going to Vereeniging where the Boers are reported to be threatening, but not attacking. You have been specially selected for this on account of your good work, during the campaign, but I hope you will shortly join me again in Johannesburg, and lastly I must congratulate you on your good conduct and smartness both in the field and camp, which has been everything to be desired. With regard to my own feelings, I may add that whatever praise or credit I may get for this campaign, I shall always remember a great deal of it is due by Colonel Spens and the Shropshires."

The following order was published by Major-General Smith Dorrien, Commanding the 19th Brigade dated 6th June, 1900: "The 19th Brigade has achieved a record of which any Infantry might be proud. Since the date it was formed, vis 12th February, it has marched 620 miles, often on half rations, seldom on full. It has taken part in the capture of 10 towns, fought in 10 general engagements, and on 27 other days. In one period of 30 days it fought on 21 of them and marched 327 miles. Casualties between 400 and 500. Defeats, NIL H. L. Smith Dorrien, Major General, Commanding 19th Brigade." The Battalion marched out of Pretoria to Irene for Vereeniging, arriving there the same night, and was resumed by march on route to a point near Mount Prospect, south of Herlbron, where a holt was made for the night.

June 9th. The outposts were attacked by De Wet, one man was severely wounded by shrapnel.

June 12th. The Battalion joined a Force under Lord Methuen, and moved off in two Columns next day, Colonel Spens commanding the one moving west of the railway, and Lord Methuen the one east. Kopje Station was reached, when the Boers under De Wet opened fire with big guns and pom-poms from the Kopjes south of the station. The Shropshires executed a brilliant movement, fighting at close quarters without any casualties. The Shropshire Yeomanry was this day met for the first time. Fighting continued until dark, and the Battalion then bivouacked close to the ground on which the 4th Derby's had their disaster on the 7th inst. Lord Methuen left next day for Kroonstad on a forced march at 3am. The Battalion then occupied Rhenoster Kopje with 6 guns and various Details of other corps.

June 13th. A small party proceeded to Roodeval Station to recover mail etc., which had been destroyed by Christian De Wet, on 7th inst. On the 13th Lord Kitchener was at Kopje Station, where he intended to remain for the night. About 3am on the 14th June De Wet opened fire on the station with his field guns, and afterwards shelled the camp. The fire was promptly replied to by our own guns. Lord Kitchener quickly left the station, and sought safety in our camp. The Boers came up to within close distance of the camp, F. Company and the Volunteer Company, under Major Doyle, repulsed them with volleys, and they were also heavily shelled when retiring, and suffered heavily. Our casualties: one man wounded.

June 18th. E and Volunteer Companies proceeded to Honing Spruit, and had only time to entrench themselves when the enemy appeared on the scene, and commenced shelling them, but no damage was done. About this time a great many comforts and various things, which had been sent out by the people of Shropshire and Herefordshire, through the help of the Countess of Powis, were received, but owing to congestion of transport, etc., could not be sent out before. These gifts were very welcome as the nights at this time were bitterly cold. The Battalion remained at Rhenester Kopjes until the 7th July, and nothing of any consequence happened during that time.

July 7th. The Battalion entrained at Kopje Station and proceeded to Irene, to rejoin the 19th Brigade (which was being formed again) and remained there till the 10th. The Battalion then proceeded to Krugersdorp with the Gordon Highlanders, under General Smith Dorrien.

July 11th. Smith Dorrien's Force marched out of Krugersdorp with 2 guns of the 20th Battery Royal Field Artillery and 20 Yeomanry. After marching for about three hours the enemy was discovered by the yeomanry to be holding a commanding position at a pass called Hekpoort. The baggage was perched on a hill in full view of the enemy, but as the General knew they had no guns it was quite safe. The Gordons advanced to the attack with two guns under Lieut. Turner, R.F. Artillery, while Companies of our Battalion were sent out on the flank of the Gordons. The Guns advanced to within 600 yards of one hill occupied by the enemy, and to within 1,800 yards of another, and opened fire with shrapnel, making splendid practice. The distance, however was too close, and before long the Boer marksmen found the range of the guns, but the gunners stuck to their work until every one of them were struck down, including the gallant Lieutenant Turner who was the last to take cover, and not even then till he was wounded in three places. Whilst this was going on in the front another act took place in the rear of the baggage, which was little less exiting,

The Boer Commander had noticed the peculiar position of the baggage, and had dispatched about 40 men to make a counter attack. As everyone had been watching the events in front the Boers approaching in the rear had been unobserved (they were partly concealed by a small ridge) until they opened fire at close range, firing directly at the baggage and transport animals. Luckily, however, no damage was done only a small stampede among the mules, and as they run the right way they gave no trouble. Captain Higginson and three men were wounded, and the enemy was successfully driven from the rear. In front, however, things were not so successful the enemy having splendid cover. The Gordons had expended all their ammunition and volunteers of A and F Companies of ours replenished their supply as well as they could. As the guns were so close the Boers thought they had an easy capture, but they were greatly deceived. Gathering on the right flank of the Gordons they would have done considerable damage, had not our Maxim gun been brought into action and kept them back for the remainder of the day. About this time gallant attempts were made by a party of men under Captain Younger, of the Gordons, to get the guns away, but the fire, however, was too heavy, and they had to retire. Captain Younger and 3 men were severely wounded, the former dying of his wounds a few hours after. His death was greatly deplored by all ranks, as he was personally known to many. After this desultory fire was kept up till after darkness had set in. The guns were got away by the Gordons after a little exciting pull, and all ranks were thoroughly tired out. The distance back to Krugersdorp was long and the enemy was now in our rear. The General decided that we must get back, and about 10pm the start was made with a beautiful full moon to help as on our way, and perhaps it was never more needed. All through the night we marched steadily along, and to avoid the danger of being ambushed, a longer route was taken to get back. At 5 a.m. next morning lights were seen, and in a very short time we were back in the town again, and perhaps the day before could be put down as the very hardest that had ever been experienced. Everyone was thoroughly tired out. The Troops did nothing that day but rest, with the exception of the burial of the late Captain Younger, which even the most tired of men attended. Outpost duty for the next few days was all that was done, and in the meantime reinforcements in the shape of Lord Methuen and his column began to detrain at Krugersdorp.

July 19th. The Regiment formed part of Lord Methuen's Column, and marched out of Krugersdorp and encamped again near a very difficult drift. Only a small portion of the baggage could negotiate the passage before dark, and consequently the Shropshires who had crossed early, were again without blankets, and another very miserable night was experienced by both officers and men. Early next morning the march was resumed towards Oliphants Nek, in which direction the enemy, under Commander Du Plessie was retiring, The march was over a good road, and through a picturesque district, well wooded with a high ridge of kopjes on the right flank, and detached kopjes on the left. The enemy was encountered about noon, and our guns were soon in action, the Shropshires moving out in skirmishing order on the right flank, and advancing along the difficult sides of the kopjes. Had a splendid view of the whole fight. Long range volleys were fired, which slowly drove the Boers from the heights and put them in motion towards the Nek. Lord Methuen pressed slowly, as a British Force under Baden Powell was expected to arrive at the Nek. The enemy, however, was seen to be moving through, and all that our Forces could do was to shell them from the plain and then follow on. On our arrival at the Nek, Baden Powell was there with his Force, some two hours late, and Du Plessie Force had escaped. The Commander himself was wounded and died at Rustenburg a few days later. Our casualties, nil. The whole force camped near the Nek, and rested next day (Sunday) Here a plentiful supply of oranges was obtained.

July 22nd. Boschfontein was reached. The following Divisional Order was published: "The Lieutenant General (Lord Methuen) has brought to the notice of the Field Marshall Commander-in-Chief the admirable way in which the Troops have carried out their very hard work during the last few days. Lord Methuen congratulates the Division that its task has been carried out at so small cost of life."

July 24th. Reached Hartebeefontein.

July 26th. Bank Station. A draft from England under Lieutenant Garsia joined the Battalion this day.

July 29th. The Battalion moved towards Potchefstroom, and arrived at Frederickstad on Tuesday, 30th, whilst the Force under General Smith Dorrien was entering the camp, a train with supplies and another draft for the Battalion, together with men who had been wounded in previous actions and men who had been left down country through sickness, was derailed in close proximity, with awful results—13 men of the Battalion were killed and 41 injured.

An unfortunate accident with considerable loss of life occurred on the way. A heavy train of supplies passed just as the column was reaching camp at Frederikstad on July 30th, and seated on the train was a draft which had lately arrived in the country, together with some sick men re-joining. Our Yeomanry scouts had been ordered to inspect the line as they advanced but they failed to perceive that on a sharp curve, where the line run down an incline, some of the fishplates had been unscrewed and the rails loosened but carefully replaced. The engine was derailed, and the heavy supply trucks run up one on top of the other. 13 KSLI men were killed together with the engine driver, 41 injured. Capt. W. S. R. Radcliffe Lieut. Dorrien Smith and Lieut. H. P. Harrid-Edge had a narrow escape having shortly before the accident moved from the front carriage, which was completely telescoped, and into a rear carriage which was undamaged.

July 31st. The Boers attacked the camp at close range. After a short but sharp exchange of rifle fire and a few shells from our guns the enemy retired without accomplishing its object, viz. the capture of a large convey, which was being loaded up for Lord Methuen's Column which was at Potchefstroon.

August 3rd. Half Battalion and Headquarters marched to Welverdiend to occupy the station there. Several days were spent in fortifying the place and outpost duty, as well as several journeys by night to Bank Station, and back again to Welverdiend. De Wet was expected to cross the line hereabouts as he was being hotly pursued by a large Mounted Force from the Free State.

August 12th. The Shropshires now formed part of a Force under Lord Kitchener in pursuit of De Wet who crossed the line about midnight on the 12th. inst., blowing up several culverts during the passage. This was a short march, because of difficult drafts.

August 13th. On the move again at 3 a.m. across a waterless and burnt country. A Brigade Order was published for information: Lord Kitchener wishes to express his appreciation of the splendid march made by the infantry, which covered 25 miles in 12 1/2 hours.

August 15th. On to Leefontein De Wet had escaped through Oilphants Nek. A Brigade order was published for information: Colonel Hoare, with some 300 bushmen and Rhodesion Horse, have held out against Delarey's Commando for over a week, some 10 miles from here, and to relieve them the General Officer Commanding is forced to call on the Troops for one more arduous march commencing at 4 a.m. He hopes that before going the full distance the Mounted Troops may report that the Boers had retired, in which case this Force will be allowed to camp at the nearest water. No words can describe the G.O.C.'s pride at the splendid way the Infantry have marched. It has drawn forth the admiration of the Mounted Troops. After a distance of 12 miles had been covered, news was brought of the retirement of the enemy, and we encamped near the scene of this heroic defence (Brakfontein).

August 16th and 17th. The Force rested.

August 18th. Moved towards Margata Pass, and thence to Rustenburg which was reached on the 19th inst. At 5 a.m. the Battalion marched towards Commando's Nek. No fighting was done, although the country was most suitable for Boer tactics.

August 21st. Camped at Wolhuter's Nek. The Battalion had now marched 75 miles in four days.

August 22nd. Battalion marched to Koos Mamagalia, a large and prettily situated Kaffie village, with a missionary and mission house. Here plenty of eggs, fowl and pigs were bought by the Troops, which were very cheap.

August 23rd. Commenced march to Pretoria, camping at Nitzicht, and reached Pretoria on the 26th without any important incidents.

August 27th. The Battalion paraded for medical inspection, and the Medical Officer found the men in a very healthy condition, with the exception of a few, although many were footsore. The Battalion was recommended for a few days' rest. Whilst resting, cloths, boots, and shirts were issued, and articles of equipment which were damaged were exchanged.

August 29th. The Battalion entrained by companies for Belfast, arriving between the 1st and 4th September. Performing outpost duty, camped alongside our old friends the Gordons.

September 5th. Escorted a convoy to Carolina, arriving there on the 6th, the Force consisting of the Suffolks, our Battalion and a Naval detachment with a 4.7 gun.

September 9th. The enemy, estimated at 500 strong, with 3 guns, was reported to be in detachments along the Kloofs of the Komati River. The Ermelo Commando (about the same strength) was believed to be near Warm-baths on the Natal-Barberton road. Our Column moved at 5.30 a.m., by Buffalo Spruit, towards Silverkop, a very difficult country for transport. About noon the enemy was discovered having taken up a commanding position on each side of the road. The Suffolk Regiment was Advance Guard and approached to within rifle range, and remained there while the guns shelled the enemy among the rocks. Two Companies of ours passed through the Suffolks and boldly advanced to the kopjes held by the Boers, and fixing bayonets, prepared the charge, but the enemy left hurriedly, enabling the while Force to advance without further opposition. Camped at Buffalo Spruit.

September 10th. Column paraded at 6.20 a.m. and moved by Warmbaths across Komati River, to Hlomhlom, without opposition. Forming the advance guard the Battalion marched towards the pass on the Barberton Road. The enemy had occupied the high kopjes on each side of the pass, and our guns were soon in action, the Royal Horse Artillery making good practice on the Boer position. E and F Companies had a very difficult climb on the right flank and were subjected to a desultory fire from the enemy at long range without loss. Having gained the heights overlooking the Pass, the enemy retired, and their lagger could be seen making hurried preparations for flight. On account of the difficulty experienced in getting guns up the Pass the enemy was enabled to get all their wagons, etc., away, with the exception of 5 wagons, which H. Company under Captain R. Gubbins, captured. Pursuit was hopeless as the whole of our convey was at the bottom of the Pass. The Naval gun alone required nearly 100 oxen to draw it up the hill of the Pass. Two Infantry Battalions furnished large fatigue parties by reliefs, both day and night, to assist the animals at difficult points. Just as the carcasses of the oxen and mules which had died from exhaustion were becoming most offensive, the last wagon was drawn up, and a hard earned rest, especially for the animals followed.

September 19th. The Force moved towards Barberton, camping on the plain, within sight of the town.

September 20th. After a hard march, the Battalion camped outside the town of Barberton, which is prettily situated at the foot of the hills. The Shropshire L.I. was detailed to garrison the town, and a pleasant and much needed rest for a month was given, only outpost duty and guard being done.

September 30th. Notification was received that Corporal A. Peel had been promoted to a Commission in the West India Regiment.

October 9th. A draft of 100 NCOs and men under Lieutenants Wrench and Payn arrived from England.

October 11th. Orders were received that the Battalion would proceed by train to Pretoria, but the destination was changed to Belfast, which place was reached on the 17th. Major General Smith Dorrien commanded the Garrison, which included the Gordon Highlanders, Royal Irish Regiment, a portion of the 5th Lancers, two Companies of Mounted Infantry, and a Battery of Royal Field Artillery.

October 18th. The Volunteer Company left the Battalion and proceeded down country by rail en route for England. The Company had a very hearty send-off by the remainder of the Battalion and was addressed by Colonel Spens before leaving.

October 19th. Brigade Order was published for information: "The General Officer Commanding cannot let the Volunteer Company of the Shropshire L.I., leave his Command for home without thanking them for all their good and hard work they have done throughout the campaign. He wishes them a safe and speedy journey, and is sure they will receive the warm welcome in the Old County which their good work at the front has merited."

October 23rd. This day the Garrison had a holiday to attend athletic sports.

November 1st. The Battalion paraded at 5 a.m. and formed part of a Force under Major-General Smith Dorrien, which had the object the capture of a Boer Laager near Caroline. The Force was divided into two parts, Colonel Spens commanding our portion, which took a circuitous route with the object of heading the enemy off. The weather however was terrible and a most wretched night was experienced, and the Force was obliged to halt at Van Wyk's Vlei until daybreak, and then return to Belfast, soaked to the skin. And thoroughly tired out, having been on the move for 16 hours.

November 3rd. The following telegraph was received from the Commander in Chief: "I am much concerned to hear of the very trying march yours and Colonal Spens Columns had, and earnestly hope the Troops have not suffered, Thursday night was bad enough here, it must have been terrible where you are. It was evidently a well conceived affair, and it is most unfortunate its complete success was married by bad weather."

November 6th. The Battalion paraded at 3 a.m. and marched towards Carolina. The Force consisted of Canadian Dragoons, Canadian Artillery, Canadian Mounted Rifles, 5th Lancers, and our Battalion. The enemy was met at Lilliefontein in a very strong position, and some very stubborn fighting ensued. Our casualties were 6 killed and 14 wounded.

November 10th. The following extract from the Summary of News was published : "Smith-Dorrien's Force had also been heavily engaged yesterday. It moved out from Belfast and was very soon opposed to the Boers, who hung on to its flanks and eventually took up a strong position, from which, however, they were forced to retire. All day signal fires were to be seen, and the following day the Boers were heavily reinforced. Our casualties on the 6th were 6 killed and 20 wounded, chiefly Shropshires who fought gallantly. The following day the Boers tried to seize again the position from which they had been driven yesterday but were driven back by the Canadian Mounted Rifles. No praise is to high for gallantry shown by the Canadian Dragoons and Artillery. Casualties this day 2 killed and 12 wounded. The following telegram was received from Lord Roberts: "You seem to have had two most successful days with the enemy, and I congratulate you and all your Troops on the admirable way in which operations were carried out." On the return of the Battalion to Belfast, the Gordons, who had previously buried our dead and carefully attended to our wounded, showed marked sympathy on the occasion of the losses sustained at Lilliefontein, and provided us with tea which was eagerly drunk by the tired and thirsty Troops. The following letter was received from then in reply to one thanking them for the kindness shown on the present occasion. "Your kind letter received and communicated to the Battalion. We are glad to know that any little effort of ours to show respect and sympathy for those in bereavement, who have been so long our comrades in arms, has been appreciated. May the good feeling and respect which prompted us to do any such action long continue, and may it ever be the good fortune of the Gordons when hard work has to be done, to have such a gallant Regiment by their side as the Shropshires."

December 9th. The Battalion, consisting of A, B, E, and G Companies, paraded to take part in a flying column under Colonel Spens. The Boers were threatening Barberton, and it appeared, if we threatened Carolina, the enemy would leave the vicinity of Barberton and come and defend Carolina, The movement commenced by a reconnaissance in force by the 5th Lancers on the 8th. The news reached the Boers who were in front of Barberton, probably by signal fires. On the 9th General Stephenson wired that the Boers were retiring from Barberton, and on the 10th they had all gone, so, the scheme worked well. Spens Force marched back during the night to avoid a rear-guard action.

December 24th. The following Battalion Orders was published: "The Commanding Officer in wishing the Regiment the Compliments of the Season, takes the opportunity of thanking all ranks for their magnificent conduct in many days of hardship throughout the year. Their endurance in long marches on short rations, bravery under fire, and the high discipline and good spirit shown on all occasions has been most highly commented on by every General under whose command the Battalion has been placed. The Commanding Officer feels justly proud of having had the honour to command such a Regiment and wishes everyone a happy return to their homes when their term of military service expires."

December 25th. The Battalion paraded for Divine Service, and a pint of beer was issued to each man for Xmas dinner. Unfortunately, the plum pudding ordered for the Troops were not forthcoming owing to the train being blown up by Jack Hindon and his men. The train also contained our Xmas mail, which was purloined as well.

December 26th. A, B, C, and H Companies paraded at 3 a.m. in Fighting Order for a reconnaissance and foraging duty. The enemy was encountered at Witport, and some desultory firing took place. Private Bayless was severely wounded and eventually died of his wounds.

December 29th. E, F, G, and H Companies under Major Bulman proceeded to Helvetia to garrison the town.

January 7th 1902. The Boers attacked Belfast, being favoured by a dense mist, some very hard fighting occurred at Monument Hill and Colliery Hill, occupied respectively by the Royal Irish Regiment and a Company of ours. The Royal Irish at Monument Hill were completely surprised (several men being killed in their beds). A large proportion of the Royal Irish was killed and wounded while the remainder were taken prisoners, being overwhelmed by superior numbers. The Colliery Hill magazine, being garrisoned by a section of B Company of ours, under Lieutenant Marshall, held out for a considerable time. The Boers eventually rushed it. Two men were killed, 2 died from wounds and 3 others were wounded, including Lieutenant Marshall. All ammunition being expended, the remainder had to surrender. The Boers treated the prisoners well and released them at Middleburg. The posts of the Gordons south of the line, were also attacked, but the Gordons, who had heard Colliery and Monument firing, were prepared for them, and the Boers had a rather a warm time of it. The attempt to capture Belfast had failed, and the Boers received a severe lesson, although the Royal Irish and the Shropshires had to mourn the loss of several brave men.

January 12th. Brigade Order was published: "The General wishes to express his appreciation of the steadiness of the Troops on the morning of the 8th, He would especially mention the fine defense of the Royal Irish picquet at Monument Hill (under that gallant officer Captain Fosbery, whose death he deplores). Overwhelmed by vastly superior numbers after a hard fight, also that of the Shropshires under Lieutenant Marshall. He regrets the heavy loss, but does not consider them heavy, considering the determined nature of the attack. He also considers, that had it not been for the heavy mist the attack would have been much more easily repulsed.

January 13th. The following telegram was received from the Assistant Adjutant-General, Middleburg: "The General wishes to convey to all ranks his thorough appreciation of their gallant conduct during the attack on the morning of the 8th."

January 18th. Forces Order No 5., of this day notifies that "Lieut. Col Spens and Lieutenant Marshall were especially mentioned in the General Officer Commanding's report on the attack of the 7th and 8th inst."

January 22nd. Force Order notifies that "Lieut-Colonel J. Spens (with local rank of Colonel) takes over command to-day at Wonderfontein of the Infantry Brigade, under General Smith Dorrien. The Brigade will be known as Spens Brigade.

January 23rd. It is with the greatest regret and sorrow that the General Officer Commanding has announce the death of Her Most Gracious Majesty, the Queen which occurred yesterday at 6.30pm.

January 24th. At noon all flags were hoisted to the masthead, and a Royal Salute of 21 guns was fired for His Majesty's accession.

January 25th. Flags hoisted half-mast, and a salute of 81 guns fired during the funeral of the late Queen Victoria.

April 3rd. The entire Battalion entrained for Wonderfontein en route to Carolina, arriving there on the 6th. The 2nd Volunteer Company having been delayed on their way to the coast left the Battalion for England on the 24th April after a year's service in South Africa.

May 5th. The following extracts from the *London Gazette*, dated 19th April, were published: "To be Companion of the Most Honourable Order of the Bath, Lieutenant Colonel J. Spens (2nd Shropshire L.I.). To be Aide-de-Camp to the King with the Brevet rank of Colonel; Lieutenant Colonel J. Spens, C. B. To be a Companion of the Distinguished Service Order; Captain and Adjutant C. P. Higginson (2nd King's Shropshire L.I.). Medal for Distinguished Conduct in the Field, Sergeant Marsden (2nd King's Shropshire L.I.).

6th May. Lieut. Colonel A. H. J. Doyle Joined from the 1st KSLI India, to take command of the Battalion.

***

In the second phase of the war, four officers and two men gained mention in despatches by Lord Kitchener for excellent work, and in his final despatch, he added the names of three officers and four non-commissioned officers and men. When peace was finally signed at Vereeniging on 1 June 1902, the regiment was in a very fit condition after all its marching and was able to return to Ladysmith and prepare for another tour of duty.

The stark official reports that record of the confrontations of the Second Battalion of the King's Shropshire Light Infantry dealt with whilst on active service in South Africa during the Boer War fails to provide a wider descriptive picture of life or death in an inhospitable, semidesert country and against a resourceful enemy. Even, today the battlefields that the Second Battalion fought over are in the same condition as in 1900 and 1901. To give some additional information regarding the trials and tribulations of the Second Battalion Shropshire Light Infantry, the following report is of great interest.

Lieut. Colonel Spens and the Officers of the 85th King's Shropshire Light Infantry beg to thank most heartily all those who have contributed in any way to send out Warm Clothing, Tobacco, or any other Articles for the Benefit of the men of the Regiment, now serving in South Africa. The generous Gifts have been most thoroughly appreciated by all ranks and are evidence of the deep interest taken by all in the doings of the Territorial Regiment. Owing to the difficulty of Transport, and to the fact that the Regiment has hardly been stationary for more than one day at any one place during the last three months, many bales of clothing, etc have not yet reached the Battalion. I regret very much to tell all concerned that the Mails, Parcels, Registered letters etc. to the Regiment which were despatched from England on or about the 6th, 13th, 20th, and 27th April and on the 5th May were burnt by the Boers at Roodeval Spruit on the 7th June.

—Lt Col. James Spens, *Wellington Journal*, Saturday, 4 August 1900

With weeping and with laughter,
Still the story told,
How well Horatius kept the bridge,
In the brave days of old.
From the Lays of Ancient Rome

2nd Battalion King's Shropshire Light Infantry Officers and NCO's in
South Africa. Courtesy of Shropshire Museum Soldiers.

Site of the Boer Laager Paardeburg. Photo taken by the author.

The Boer Memorial at Paardeburg. Photo taken by the author

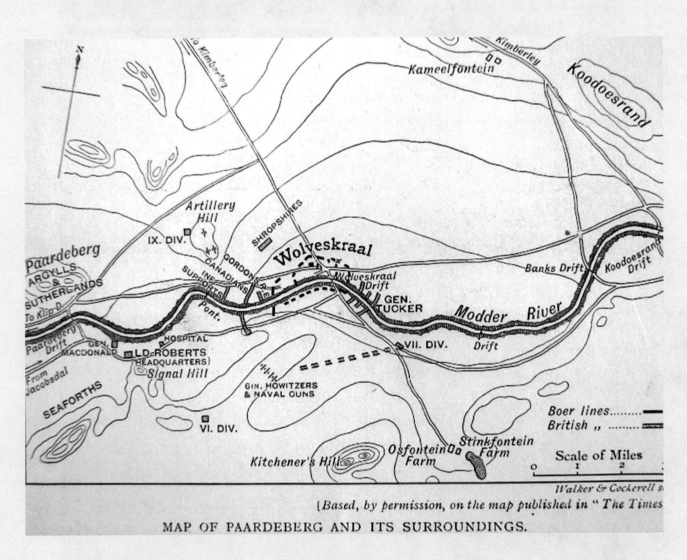

MAP OF PAARDEBERG AND ITS SURROUNDINGS.

[Based, by permission, on the map published in "The Times

Image from Alamy.

4th Battn M I

Lieut. H. M. Smith, The King's (Shropshire) L. I.

To have the Distinguished Conduct Medal

Coldstream Guards

Clr. Sgt. J. Gardham (now Sgt. Major, K. S. L. I.)

Casualties for October 1901

Increase - nil

Decrease :-

To England - 3.

To Army Reserve in South Africa - 3.

Died of wounds received in Action at Lydenburg 9.10.01
— No. 5653 Pt. Boothman

2.11.01

Orders were issued that a trench 3 feet deep by
3 feet wide was to be started so as to make a
continuous trench fro from station to station, also
a barbed wire fence. The object of this was to
prevent the Boers crossing the Railway Line at night,
for at this time of the year it was very misty, especially
around Belfast, which enabled the Boers to cross more
easily. The Block houses in some cases being a
considerable distance apart Each man in the Block
House had to work for 2½ hours daily in addition to
his other duties

About this time a local Company of M I was
formed by Mjr. C. T. Dawkins. C M G, purely of
Volunteers, from men of the Battalion, its object was
to make night raids on the town and its surroundings
to try & capture, if possible, any Boers that might
come in after dark for food etc.

11.11.01

Musician K Mills was granted the medal for
long Service and Good Conduct

Fourth Battalion King's Shropshire Light Infantry Records Book, 8 June 1900. Shropshire Archives.

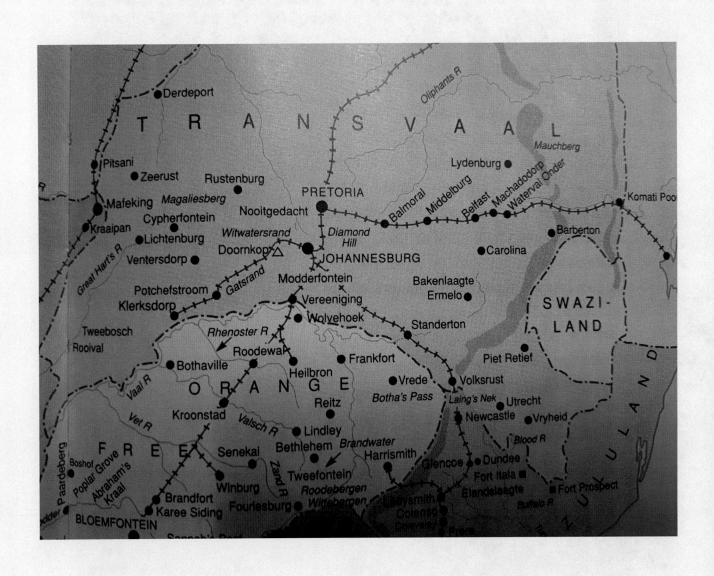

Image courtesy of the Soldiers of Shropshire Museum.

THE SECOND BATTALION KING'S SHROPSHIRE LIGHT INFANTRY

When hostilities ceased on 1 June 1902, records show that during the Boer War, the battalion had lost a total of 146 officers, non-commissioned officers, and men who were killed in action or died from disease. In addition, the battalion had 13 officers and 134 non-commissioned officers and men wounded throughout the war, and those incapacitated by illness during the war would have been in their hundreds.

The battalion consisted of the following.

- Regular enlisted officers and other ranks
- Regular enlisted sick and wounded in hospital in England
- Reserve regulars called to the colours for the duration of the war
- Old Special Service regulars (company strength)
- First Battalion King's Shropshire Light Infantry Company from India
- Fourth Battalion King's Shropshire Light Infantry (Herefordshire Militia) company strength
- Volunteer Service Company (Shropshire/Herefordshire) company strength
- Sick and wounded from attached companies

Whilst arrangements were being made for the return and transport these additional companies to England and India, the battalion also received orders for its transfer from South Africa to India during the India Relief Transfer Season, from October 1902 to March 1903. The order of movement that I have been able to find follows.

A draft of the Second Battalion King's Shropshire Light Infantry departed Southampton on 9 December 1902 aboard *Syria*, consisting of three officers, two warrant officers, three sergeants, one corporal, and eighty-nine privates and boys, as well as the women and children of the battalion. They were at Las Palmas on 15 December and at Cape Town on 31 December. The Battalion embarked at Durban for India per the SS *Syria* and left Durban on 10 January 1903. The strength of the battalion was eleven officers, thirty-six sergeants, thirty-two corporals, fourteen buglers, and 341 privates, and they arrived at Bombay on 24 January 1903. The battalion was stationed at Ranikber, Bengal.

Two officers, four sergeants, one bugler, three corporals, and forty men of B Company were left behind at Natal owing to there being no accommodation on the SS *Syria*. There were also two buglers and forty-six men of the battalion left in South African hospitals.

The steamship *Dilware* left Point Natal on 10 March and had on board eighteen NCOs and men from Second Shropshire King's Light Infantry. Troops and details for India would trans ship at Colombo and proceed under local arrangements.

Courtesy of the Emily Hobhouse Museum, Bloemfontein.

During the Anglo-Boer War, several battles and skirmishes took place in and around Belfast, The railway line run from Pretoria to the Port of Maputo on the coast of Portuguese West Africa. Belfast has a subtropical climate with mild summers and chilly dry winters.

The occupation of Pretoria June 5th—troops passing before Lord Roberts—S. Africa.
Copyright 1901 by Underwood & Underwood.

2nd Battalion King;s Shropshire Light Infantry marching in in Pretoria.

**The little green tents where the Soldiers sleep,
and the sunbeams play and the women weep,
are covered with flowers today.**

—Walt Mason

Shipping to and from the Boer War

A great source of information regarding the movement of members of the Second Battalion of the King's Shropshire Light Infantry were the shipping records to and from South Africa. These records also provide other interesting aspects about the Boer War.

London Times, 8 November 1899: "The ARAWA departed Southampton the 7th Nov. with the 2/Shropshire Light Infantry 29 Officers and 752 men. For South Africa. Arrived Cape Town Friday 5th December 1899."

London Times, 22 December 1899: "The *Jelunga* departed Southampton 21st Dec. with drafts for the 2/ Shropshire Light Infantry, Lt. English, 2/Lt Dele-Murray, and 175 men. Arrive Cape Town 18th January 1900."

Southampton, 25 February 1900: "The *Assaye* also sailed today with 81 Officers and 2007 men, Shropshire Light Infantry, 2/Lt. C. A. Howard.

Wellington Journal, Saturday, 14 April 1900:

> The 4th Battalion of the Shropshire Regiment (Herefordshire Militia), Which has been embodied since the commencement of the war under the command of Colonel Lucas, and was at stationed at Gravesend, is now at Tipperary and a draft of the line recruits left Shrewsbury to the battalion on Tuesday. The 4th Shropshire have sent 100 rank and file of their reserves to reinforce the Line Regiment in South Africa,
>
> During the week two more drafts of retired Shropshire soldiers who have re-joined this new branch of the service for a period of 12 months have been despatched from the Shrewsbury Barracks, their destination being Newport and Pembroke. The total number who have re-joined at Shrewsbury is about 250.
>
> The *Kildonan Castle* left Cape Town the 25th April 1900 for England with Sick and Wounded. 2/Shropshire Light Infantry Lt. Atchinson. Sick laying down 45, Sick convalescent 206, Wounded laying down 29, Wounded convalescent 21.
>
> The *Servia* with invalids from South Africa arrived Southampton 10th May 1900, 2/ Shropshire Light Infantry Lt. H. M. Smith, the *Servia* brought 150 men.

London Times, 26 May 1900:

> The *Canada* left for England 17th May, with the following. 2/Shropshire Light Infantry. 2/Lt. Kettlewell. Sick laying down 94, Sick convalescent 396, Wounded laying down 23, Wounded convalescent 25.

> The *Montfort* left Cape Town 31st May 1900, and had the following on board, 2nd Shropshire Light Infantry Lt. ATCHISON, Sick laying down 18 Sick convalescent 250, Wounded laying down 2, Sick convalescent 2. Arrive Plymouth 25 June.

London Times, 6 June 1900: "The *Canada* arrived Southampton the 5th. 2/Shropshire Light Infantry 2/Lt. Kettlewell, 545 men sick and wounded 1 death on voyage."

London Times, 8 June 1900:

> The *Aurana* arrived at Queenstown yesterday for South Africa and embarked 1 Officer and 100 Light Infantry, men of the 2/Shropshire

> The *Canada* left for England 1st, August 1900, with sick and wounded Shropshire Light Infantry. 2Lt. Carter and Miles. Sick laying down 39. Sick convalescent 857, Wounded laying down 13, wounded convalescent 64.

Wellington Journal, 4 August 1900:

> Lieut. Colonel SPENS and the Officers of the 85th King's Shropshire Light Infantry beg to thank most heartily all those who have contributed in any way to send out Warm Clothing, Tobacco, or any other Articles for the Benefit of the men of the Regiment, now serving in South Africa. These generous Gifts have been most thoroughly appreciated by all ranks and are evidence of the deep interest taken by all in the doings of the Territorial Regiment. Owing to the difficulty of Transport, and to the fact that the Regiment has hardly been stationary for more than one day at any one place during the last three months, many bales of clothing, etc have not yet reached the Battalion. I regret very much to tell all concerned that the Mails, Parcels, Registered letters etc to the Regiment which were despatched from England on or about the 6th, 13th, 20th, and 27th April and on the 5th May were burnt by the Boers at Roodeval Spruit on the 7th June.
>
> —Lt Col. James Spens

London Times, 17 August 1900: "The *Aurania* arrived at Queenstown yesterday from Southampton en route to Cape Town, she will embark the following today, 27 Officers and 1032 men. 2nd Shropshire Light Infantry 2 officers Lt. Payne and Lt. Wrench and 100 men. Arrived at Cape Town on the 6th September 1900."

London Times: "The TROJAN left for England 24th September 1900, with Sick and Wounded. 2/Shropshire Light Infantry QM. Forrest. Sick laying down, Sick convalescent 32."

London Times, 25 September 1900: "The transport *Suffolk* has gone ashore 20 miles west of Cape Saint Francis. West of Port Elizabeth and was sinking, the *Lake Erie* is standing by. The *Suffolk* sank with the loss of 800 animals no loss of humans."

London Times, 1 October 1900: "The *Trojan* left Cape Town 24th September with Sick and Wounded. 2/ Shropshire Light Infantry QM Forrest."

Gloucester Citizen, 2 November 1900: "The 4th Battalion King's Shropshire Light Infantry, returned to Hereford on Thursday, after a stay of ten or eleven months in training and camp quarters at Gravesend, Tipperary, Kilworth, and Waterford."

London Times, 1 December 1900: "The *Nineveh* arrived Plymouth yesterday with the following invalids. Shropshire Light Infantry, Major Reade."

London Times, 5 December 1900: "The *Assaye*, arrived Southampton yesterday with the following invalids, 2/Shropshire Light Infantry, Capt. J. J. White."

London Times, 5 December 1900: "The *Fort Salisbury* arrived Plymouth with the following passengers, Vol Com Shropshire Light Infantry Lt Edge. Wounded Laying down 11, convalescent 20."

London Times, 11 March 1901: "The *Catalonia* left 7th March Cape Town with invalids 2/ Shropshire Light Infantry Lt. C. Marshall, Sick laying down 50, Convalescent 355."

London Times 15th March 1901. The *Malta* from Albert Dock with Volunteer Company Shropshire Light Infantry

London Times, 25 March 1901: "The *Suedic* on the 23rd from Liverpool, 3 Officers and 110 men. Shropshire Light Infantry."

London Times, 11 April 1901: "The *Orotava* left for England 5th with the following invalids Sick Laying Down 7, Convalescent 180, Wounded Laying Down 11, Convalescent 8, Passage home, Volunteer Company Shropshire Light Infantry Lt. J. F. Cutler, and 1000-time expired men."

London Times, 15 April 1901: "The *Formosa* left Cape Town 10th with Volunteer Company Shropshire Light Infantry, Lt. B. Head and 93 men. Arrived Southampton 7th May."

London Times, 16 April 1901: "The *Manhatten* left Albert Docks 15th. Shropshire Light Infantry Lt. C. A. Wilkinson."

London Times, 3. July 1901: "The *Orotava* arrived Southampton last night with invalids. Shropshire Light Infantry Lt. E. R. M. English, and Lt R. C. Middleton."

Date Line London, 26 June 1901: "Army pensions for widows has been set in amounts of 13 to 30 pounds per annum."

London Times, 23 July 1901: "The *Victorian* arrived Queenstown Sunday night Embarked Shropshire Light Infantry 3 Officers and 325 men sailed for South Africa."

London Times, 15 August 1901: "The *Avoca* left Natal for England with invalids. 2/Shropshire Light Infantry Capt. R. A. Smith and R. R. Gibbins."

London Times, 23 August 1901: "The *Orcana* arrived at Plymouth with invalids. 2/Shropshire Light Infantry. Major A. R. Austen. home 840 men included several Imperial Yeomen rejected not able to ride or shoot."

London Times, 27 August 1901: "The Assaye arrived Southampton."

London Times: The *Mohawk* left for England 30th September 1901 with the following invalids. Sick laying down 9. Convalescent 641, Wounded 1, convalescent 9.

London Times, 31 October 1901: "The *Canada* left for England Oct. 24th. With invalids. 2/Shropshire Light Infantry 2/Lt. R. A. K. Wilson. Wounded laying down 29 convalescent 12. Sick laying down 65, convalescent 396."

London Times, 21 November 1901: "The hospital ship *Simla* left for England 14th Nov. Sick laying Down 102, convalescent 139 wounded laying down 18, convalescent 15. 2/Shropshire Light Infantry. 2/Lt. W. L. Herd."

London Times, 23 December 1901: "The Bavarian left on the 17th Dec. for England with invalids. Sick laying down 40, convalescent, 426, wounded laying down 16, convalescent 20. 2/Shropshire Light Infantry Capt. C. J. GARSIA."

London Times, 4 January 1902: "Hospital Ship *The Dunera* left for England 20th December with invalids. 2/Shropshire Light Infantry Lt. J. M. Carter. Sick Laying Down 3, convalescent 245, Wounded laying down 5 convalescent 32."

London Times, 29 January 1902: "The *Roslin Castle* left for England with the following invalids Sick laying down 3, convalescent 439, wounded convalescent 11, 2/Shropshire Light Infantry Lt. E. A. Underwood."

London Times, 24 February 1902:

The *Gaika* left for England 19th. Feb. with the following. 4/Shropshire Light Infantry. 2.L/t E. R. Cox., The Ship carried 625 men.

The *Dunera* left for England 14th March 1902 with invalids, Sick laying down 18, convalescent 247, Wounded laying down 3. Convalescent 16. 2/Shropshire Light Infantry. Capt. J. G. Forbes.

The *Britanic* left for England 21st April 1902 4th Shropshire Light Infantry L/t F. H. Hemingway

London Times. 17 May 1902: "The *Lake Erie* left for England 12 May with passengers. VC 2/Shropshire Light Infantry, Capt. B. W. Treasure, L/t P. Anthony and 95 men. To Southampton."

London Times, 16 June 1902: "The *Nubia* arrived at Southampton yesterday bringing 251 invades for Netley, 29 for Aldershot, 72 for convalescent Camp, and 98 for Fort Brockhurst."

London Times, 24 June 1902: "The *Orotava* left for England 23rd. with Lord Kitchener, and General French."

London Times, 28 June 1902: "St. Helena, 27th. The first batch of Boer Prisoners to return home 478, sailed from here yesterday (Ship The Canada)."

London Times, 8 July 1902: "The *Dunotter Castle* left for England 2nd. July with the following passenger for home. 2/Shropshire Light Infantry Colonel J. Spens and Major C. H. E. Marescaux."

London Times, 9 July 1902: "The *Avoca* left Point Natal for England, Shropshire Light Infantry 6th July with the following invalid's L/t G. F. Mallor and C. M. Smith. And 540 Invalides men."

Hereford Journal, 12 July 1902: "The Hereford Militia, The strength of the Regiment on its return was only about 300 men, but it must be remembered that about 25 men who have lately returned from South Africa are "on Leave", and about 80 men have not yet come home."

London Times, 9 August 1902: "The *Saxon* left Cape Town for Southampton 31st. with the following. 2/Shropshire Light Infantry, Capt. H. Hudson, L/t Huth and 107 men.".

Shrewsbury Chronicle, 15 August 1902:

RESERVISTS COMING HOME—The SS *Saxon* carrying Captain H. Hudson, Lieutenant P. C. Huth and 103 reservists of the 2nd, King's Shropshire Light Infantry from South Africa, is due to arrive in Southampton tomorrow (Saturday) and the men are expected in Shrewsbury the same day. The Mayor of Shrewsbury (Mr S. Meeson Morris) has issued a notice expressing the hope that the inhabitants will honour the occasion by decorating their premises on the road from the station, up Castle street, Pride-Hill and Mardol to Copthorne Barracks. The men will be welcomed on behalf of the town by the Mayor and Corporation, who will entertain them with refreshments in addition to the ordinary rations with which they will be supplied at the Barracks.

Shrewsbury Chronicle, 15 August 1902:

MILITARY INTELLIGENCE. From Fridays *London Gazette*

The King's (Shropshire) Light Infantry, Bt. Col. J. Spens C. B. aide-de-camp to his Majesty, from supernumerary Lieutenant-Colonel is placed on half-pay.

London Times, 20 August 1902: "The *Arundel Castle* left for England 4th Aug. with passengers for home. Shropshire Light Infantry Captains E. R. Luard and H. G. Bryant. 2/Lt. F. J. Leach. And 149 men."

London Times, 26th August 1902: "The *Plassy* left for England 19th. Shropshire Light Infantry. Lt. B. L. Williams."

London Times, 27 August 1902:

The *Orcana* left for England 21st with invalids Shropshire Light Infantry Capt. H. M. Smith, Sick laying down 42, convalescent 247, wounded laying down 6 convalescents.

The *Dunvegan Castle* left for England 20th Aug. Shropshire Light Infantry Major C. T. Dawkins, Lt G. A. Delme-Murray, and 99 men.

Wellington Journal, 6 September 1902:

More Shropshire reservists coming home. Until the arrival of the *Dunvegan Castle* at Southampton which is due in the course of to-day, nothing can be said for certain as to the hour Major Dawkins and his party of 100 men of the Shropshire regiment will arrive at Shrewsbury. Official intimation, however, will reach Colonel Robinson in the usual course, and will once be made known to the town. Arrangements are also being made for a telegram to be sent from Southampton to the Shrewsbury office of the journal stating the hour the troops will leave for Shrewsbury. Major Dawkins's contingent will include a number of men who joined from the 1st battalion in India at the end of last year, and who are due to discharge to the Reserve. They are to be entertained to dinner at the Barracks this evening at the expense of the Reception Committee.

Wellington Journal, 6 September 1902:

According to a special Army Order just published regarding the Indian Reliefs, the authorities have decided that the 1st Battalion of the Shropshire Regiment in India is to come home, and the 2nd Shropshire will be moved from South Africa to India. The changes of stations are to take place between October and March. The decision will afford considerable satisfaction to the 2nd Shropshire to know that they will not form part of the South Africa garrison. According to advice by the last mail the Shropshire's were expecting to receive orders to move into Natal, evidently preparatory to embarking at Durban for India

London Times, 12 September 1902, The *Guelph* left for England 7th Sept. Shropshire Light Infantry 2/ Lt. H. B. Green.

London Times, 18 September 1902: "The *Rippingham Grange* left for England on the 14th. Shropshire Light Infantry Lt. E. P. Dorien-Smith with 68 men. Due 10th October."

Ludlow Advertiser, 20 September 1902:

The 1st Battalion King's Shropshire Light Infantry, now at Poona, India, have at last received orders to embark for England after about 19 years foreign service. On August 10th

1882 the battalion left Kingston, Ireland, for Egypt, and after taking part in the Egyptian war left Egypt for China, where they did excellent service during the plague at Hong Kong, and were awarded special medals by the government, At that time they were described as the white Wash Brigade, From China the regiment embarked for India, and during the South African war several drafts have been sent to the 2nd Battalion on active service. At present there are only three serving with the Battalion who embarked in 1882, these being Major Pearsem Sergeant, Major G. Wyild, and Lance Corporal T. Wright.

Homeward Mail from India and China and the East, 29 September 1902:

2nd Battalion Shropshire Light Infantry Departed Southampton 9th December aboard the SYRIA, Las Palmas 15th December, Cape Town 31st December, Leave Durban January 10th, arrive Bombay 24th January 1903. Station in India Ranikber, Bengal.

The *Dilwara* left for England 1st October, 1902. Shropshire Light Infantry Capt. C. W. Battye.

The *Ionian* left Point Natal 3rd October for Bombay returning Boer Escorts. 2/Shropshire Light Infantry 2/Lt. P. C. Johnson and 66 men.

Shrewsbury Chronicle, 10 October 1902:

MIDLAND TROOPS FOR INDIA

Second-Lieutenant F. C. Johnson and 66 non-commissioned officers and men of the 2nd Battalion of the Shropshire Light Infantry embarked on the SS *Ionian* at Point Natal on October 3rd for India and are due at Bombay on October 19th.

London Gazette, 31 October 1902:

To be Brevet Lt/Col, Major C. T. DAWKINS C.M.G.,

To be Brevet Major Captain WILKINSON.

Private MEREDITH, D.C.M.

Wellington Journal, 15 November 1902: "The Midland troops who are due in India include Second-Lieutenant P. D. C. Johnson and 166 of the King's Shropshire Light Infantry."

London Times, 5 December 1902:

The *Kildonan Castle* left for England 26th Nov. with the following. 2/Shropshire Light Infantry Capt. Higginson, L/t P. R. C. Groves.

The *Montrose* left for England DEC. 17th for passage home 2/Shropshire Light Infantry. Major C. A. Wilkinson, and 102 men.

Shrewsbury Chronicle, 9 January 1903: "On Monday night the SS *Montrose* reached Southampton from South Africa and disembarked most passengers on Tuesday morning. Amongst them were Major Wilkinson and about 100 men of the Shropshire Regiment. Most of whom, after being attached for a time to the details of the regiment in Ireland, are intended for service in India with the First Battalion."

Homeward Mail from India China and the East, 21 MARCH 1903: "The steamship *Dilware* left Point Natal on March 10th and have on board the following Indian drafts. 2nd Shropshire Light Infantry 18 NCOs and men. Troops and details for India will Trans-Ship at Colombo and proceed under local arrangements."

Northern Whig, 8 September 1903: "SHROPSHIRE LIGHT INFANTRY ATTACKED BY CHOLERA. Information has been received at Shrewsbury stating that the 2nd Battalion King's Shropshire Light Infantry which greatly distinguished itself at Paardsbarg and in other engagements in the late Boer War, had been attacked by cholera at Ranikbad, Bengal, and that Lt. Carter and ten men had died of the disease."

In the quarry in Shrewsbury on 22 July 1904, the following memorial was unveiled.

> To the memory of the officers, non-commissioned officers & men of the line, militia, volunteer battalions of the King's Shropshire Light Infantry
>
> Who were killed in action or died of wounds or disease whilst with the 2nd Battalion, of the King's Shropshire Light Infantry (85th)
>
> In the Transvaal, Orange River Colony, or Cape Colony during the Campaign in South Africa, 1899–1902
>
> The Memorial has been erected by their comrades, Officers, Non-Commissioned Officers and men of the Line, Militia and Volunteers Battalions of the King's Shropshire Light Infantry.

There are 146 names on the memorial, which include seven names of members of the Fourth Battalion (Herefordshire Militia) King's Shropshire Light Infantry and three names of the Herefordshire Volunteer Company.

The memorial also records that thirteen officers and 134 non-commissioned officers and men had been wounded in the South African Boer War.

**There are many kinds of sorrow
In this world of love and hate,
But there is no sterner sorrow than a
Soldier's for his mate.
—Geoffrey Studdert-Kennedy**

The King's Shropshire Light Infantry Memorial. Photo by the author.

Bills. vide
Camp Orders | for the ... bills should be settled before the 6th the following month. vide Camp Order no 3 dg gr. 5.00.

Officers leave
vide orders
dg Bgde Office
913 May 1900 | Officers wishing leave of absence for more than three days. must place their application before the Comdg officer several days in advance in order that the Brigade Major may be notified. Officers once detailed for duty will not except under very exceptional circumstances be granted any leave that will necessitate their releif.

Draft to 5
S Africa | "The undernamed N C Os & men w be held in readiness to proceed to S Afric on or about the 1st proximo. They wil paid up to and for the 25th inst and transferred to the pay of the Details the 26th inst. all documents to be in Details orderly Room by 9 am on the latte date.

A Coy. | No 1250 Sgt F Morris. No 1191 Cpl W Bull

Fourth Battalion King's Shropshire Light Infantry Records Book,
Sgt. F. Morris No 1250. Shropshire Archives.

"Shropshire Reservists Return To-Day Welcome at Shrewsbury"

—Wellington Journal, 16 August 1902

It is now nearly three years since the Reservists of the Shropshire Regiment were called up to Shrewsbury to re-join the Colours, and proceed to take part in the South African Campaign, where they have rendered splendid service. Many of the men have already returned from the seat of war, being either invalided or time expired, and have resumed their civil occupations. While the heartiest of receptions have been accorded the Yeomanry and Rifle Volunteer Companies on their return home, up to the present no opportunity has been afforded to show how deeply is appreciated the service of the Reservists who so promptly responded to the call of duty in the early part of October 1899. It will therefore afford all classes much gratification to know that they will be given the opportunity to-day (Saturday) to welcome home at Shrewsbury a first contingent of Reservists, a company consisting of Captain H. Hudson (in command) Lieutenant P. C. Huth, and 103 non-commissioned officers having left for home by the Union Castle steamer Saxon, which is due to arrive at Southampton early today, when they will be disembarked and sent on to Shrewsbury without delay for discharge. On receipt of the official information that the company would arrive by the Saxon, Colonel Robinson at once took steps to interest himself in their home-coming, the fact being communicated to the Mayor of Shrewsbury, and it has been arranged to give the men a hearty reception on their arrival. The town will also entertain them to dinner, which will be provided in the large Men's Rooms at the Barracks, where the Mayor and others will attend. Colonel Robinson will receive prompt intimation of their departure from Southampton and will take steps to make the time of their arrival known in Shrewsbury immediately he receives the news. Captain Hudson and his men will in the first place be received at the Railway Station by Colonel Robinson, and headed by the band of the 3rd Shropshire L/I. will proceed to Copthorne, via Castle Street, Pride Hill, Mardol, and Frankwell. Before receiving their discharge Colonel Robinson will undertake the interesting function of presenting the men with their medals. The detachment will consist of 50 Army Reservists, 25 Shropshire Militia Reservists, and 25 Herefordshire Militia Reservists, nearly all of whom have served throughout the whole of the war, including Paardaburg, and other principal engagements under Lord Roberts. They have enjoyed the unique experience of travelling home on the same steamer with Generals Botha, De Wet, and Delarey, the first two of whom they fought against on several occasions.

Intimation was received yesterday to the effect that the Saxon would arrive at Southampton at 5 o'clock this (Saturday) morning. It is expected therefore, that the Shropshire contingent will be in time to get away by the 9.07 a.m. train, which is due to arrive at Shrewsbury at 2.55.

Hereford Journal, 30 August 1902

The militiamen who have recently returned from the Front were on Monday evening entertained to dinner at the City and Country Dining Rooms, this kindness being extended to them through the instrumentality of Miss Maude Bull, Miss Leigh, and Col. Scobie, The company numbered about 30 and besides the guests of the evening there were present, The Dean, Col. Scobie, Capt. Symonds-Taylor, Capt. Phillips, Miss M. Bull, Miss Leigh, and Dr. DuBuisson, all of whom have evinced a lively interest in the Reservists who have been serving in South Africa, the two ladies having also done their utmost for the families which were deprived of their bread-winners during the war.

The Wellington and Shrewsbury Journal, 30 August 1902

AN OFFICERS APPRECIATION TO SHREWSBURY WELCOME

The Mayor of Shrewsbury has received the following letter from Captain Hudson, who was in command of the Reservists who reached Shrewsbury from South Africa on Saturday, the 16th inst.:

> The Dell, Cowes, Isle of Wight. August 20th 1902. Dear Mr. Mayor, I feel that the brief reply I made to your kind address of welcome to the Shropshire Reservists last Saturday, was quite inadequate, but as you had been waiting so long, and the men had had such a tiring day, I thought it best for all not to delay matters. The last year of the war has been a very tedious one. There has been nothing to enliven the monotony of blockhouse life, except the weekly arrival of the home mail and the useful gifts the county has sent us from time to time, and in the name of the Militia and the Reservists attached to the 85th I thank the people of Shropshire and of Herefordshire for the kindly and practical interest they have taken in their representatives at the front. I have no words to express how thoroughly the draft appreciated the royal welcome accorded us by the borough of Shrewsbury. I can only say that any discomforts we may have experienced in South Africa were forgotten in the joy of the home-coming.
> —Very sincerely yours, Herbert Hudson, Captain, Shropshire Militia

It was the ravages of Disease, the extremes of climate, the hostilities of the civilian population, the Boer Marksmanship and ambushes, Flies and mosquitoes, were what most British officers and men remember about the Boer War, and on their return found that the Volunteer Companies had stolen the headlines.

On the 21st March 1908 the United Kingdom paid the Boer States. Nine and a half million pounds compensation for damage done during the Anglo-Boer War 1899–1902.

.... at Galbally, and Ballylanders was
reached at 7. p.m. Camp was pitched
and the troops after camping for the night,
struck camp & resumed their march for
Kilworth at 6.30. a.m, arriving at their
destination at noon on May 4th. It left
A party of about sixty men medically unfit
for the march proceeded from Tipperary to
Kilworth Camp by train on May 3rd, under
command of Lt. Col. Bourne.
The Battalion and Details 2nd Batt. Shropsh. L.I.
were encamped at Kilworth from May 4th
to October 2nd 1900, forming part of the
Militia Brigade under the command of Brig. Gen.
H. J. A. Arthill.
During its stay at Kilworth Camp the Battalion
was exercised in musketry, field-firing,
Company field training, and in brigade
and divisional manoeuvres. The weather was
very wet & cold in May and in part of
June, July & August, but fine throughout
September. Notwithstanding the inclemency
of the weather the health of the battalion was
good.
On June 8th 40 non-commissioned officers &
men of the Battalion, belonging to the Militia Reserve
proceeded to S. Africa to join the 2nd Batt.
Shropsh. L.I.
On July 7th the battalion assembled on parade
by Col. E. S. Lucas, commdg. Volunteered for
active service in China.

With kind permission of Shropshire Archives

GLOSSARY OF BOER AND MILITARY TERMS USED IN TEXT

Argentine: a horse (remount) from Argentina

Burgher: every Boer who possesses the franchise

cape cart: small, covered, two-wheeled, horse-drawn cart

donga: a riverbed deeply eroded and often dry.

Dopper: ultraconservative sect of Dutch Reformed Church

drift: a ford through a river

enteric: typhoid

fontei: a spring

frou: wife; also used for any older Boer woman

hands opper: literally, hands uppermost; a surrendered Boer

helio: heliograph, system of signalling by reflecting sunlight

inspan: Harness up, hence outspan; unharness

Joes: soldier's term for Boers

Kaffir: African (now derogatory)

karroo: semidesert interior of old Cape Province

klip: a small stone

kloof: a mountain ravine

kopie: a small hill, often flat-topped

kraal: African village; cattle enclosure

krantz: a crown of rock on a hill; a cliff

Martini: a type of rifle with a lever action like a Winchester

Mauser: German bolt-action rifle used effectively by the Boers

MI: mounted infantry

nek: a saddle (pass) between hills

Pom-Pom: small (one-pounder) 37 mm horse-drawn, quick-firing cannon

poort: a pass between hills

RAMC: Royal Army Medical Corps

Rooinek: Boer term for British soldiers; redneck

sluit: a ditch on the veldt, usually dry

St Helena: South Atlantic island to which Boer POWs were sent

Tod Sloan: alone; cockney rhyming slang

vedette: a mounted sentry, or sentry post in general

veldt (veld): the open plains

vlei: a marsh or wetlands; a pond

W(h)aler: Australian horse, but specifically from New South Wales

REFERENCES

Information was drawn from the following sources.

The Transvaal War 1899–1900. By C.N.Robinson Publisher Geo Newnes Ltd. 1900.

The Illustrated London News, Shropshire, (Mounted Infantry).

The Boer War, 1899–1902, Tommy Atkins Letters. By P.B.Boyden. London 1990.

The Army Post Office.

Edward Spiers, *The Late Victorian Army, 1868–1914*, p. 204–205 Manchester

Murray Cosby Jackson, *A Soldier's Diary (South Africa 1899–1902)*. Publisher Max Goschen. London 1913.

Thomas Parkenham, *The Boer War*, illustrated edition. London: Weidenfeld and Nicolson, 1993.

Sheila Patterson, *The Last Trek: A Study of the Boer People and the Afrikaner Nation*. 1957.

Owen David Powell, *Snapshots from the Boer War*.

Julia Symons, *Buller's Campaign*. Publisher The Cresset Press, 1963.

Philip J. Haythornthwatte, *The Colonial War Source Book*. Publisher Arms & Armour, 1996.

Thomas Pakenham, *The Boer Bar: A Consummate Masterpiece*. Publisher Random House 1979.

H. W. Nevinson, *Ladysmith: The Diary of a Siege*. Publisher Tredition Classics 2013.

William Collins, *Hereford and the Great War*. Publisher Jakeman & Carver. Hereford, 1919.

T. J. B. Hill, *Manu Forti*. Publisher Alan Sutton. 1996.

P. K. Kemp, *The History of the 4th Battalion KSLI (TA)*. Publisher Wilding & son Shrewsbury, 1955.

The Hereford Cathedral.

Bega District News. New South Wales, Australia.

Will Bennett, *Absent-Minded Beggars*.

Royal Hospital Chelsea Library.

In-Pensioner David Lyall, Royal Hospital Chelsea.

Richard Cannon, *Historical Records of the 36th of Herefordshire Regiment of Foot*. London: Furnivall and Parker.

Record of the 2nd Battalion King's Shropshire Light Infantry, during the Campaign in South Africa 1899–1902. 5005/SHYK/10/026.

Peter Dickers, *Soldiers of Shropshire, Publisher The History Press. 1989*

Rudyard Kipling. Published by Faber and Faber. 1976.

Orange Free State Archives. South Africa.

Natal Archives. South Africa.

Transvaal Archive Depot, Pretoria. South Africa.

Lachlin Gordon-Duff, *The Gordon Highlanders: To the Boer War and Beyond*. Publisher Travis Book. 1998.

Alamy Images.

British Newspapers Archives.

AUTHOR BIOGRAPHY

The author, Ivor George Williams was born in Hereford in February 1932. His father had served in the King's Shropshire Light Infantry in the 1920's with service in the Occupation of the Rhineland Germany, and in India, and in September 1939 was recalled to the colours. Like many other families we received the War Office Telegram stating that my father was missing believed killed in France, but being an old K.S.L.I. man, my father was one of the last to be evacuated from France, in June 1940.

In 1949 I enlisted in the Welsh Guards with public duties in London and service in Germany and Berlin and in Egypt. In 1957 I migrated to Australia and was a Federal Police Officer for 32 years. With service in S.A. N.T., A.C.T., N.S.W., and Washington, U.S.A. On retirement, I established a vineyard and winery. In 2015 it was time to retire and I became a In-Pensioner at the Royal Hospital Chelsea.

Name:	Francis Morris
Gender:	Male
Rank:	LSgt
Record Type:	Disability
Birth Date:	1866
Residence Place:	Hereford
Military Service Region:	England, Midlands
Discharge Date:	2 Feb 1919
Service Number:	20582
Corps, Regiment or Unit:	Royal Defence Corps
Service Branch:	Military (Army)
Title:	WWI Pension Record Cards and Ledgers
Description:	Pension Record Ledger
Reference Number:	6/MM/No.5459
Household Members:	Name
	Francis Morris

Citation: Western Front Association, London, England; WWI Pension Record Cards and Ledgers; Refere

Printed in the United States
by Baker & Taylor Publisher Services